FROM DETERRENCE TO DEFENCE

FROM DETERRENCE TO DEFENCE

The Inside Story of Strategic Policy

Michael Charlton

HARVARD UNIVERSITY PRESS
CAMBRIDGE, MASSACHUSETTS
1987

This edition is published by arrangement with BBC Books,
a division of BBC Enterprises Ltd.

This book is printed on acid-free paper, and its binding materials
have been chosen for strength and durability.

Library of Congress Cataloging-in-Publication Data

Charlton, Michael.
  From deterrence to defence.

  Based on the author's BBC radio series, The Star
wars history.
  Includes index.
  1. United States—Military policy.   2. Nuclear
warfare.   3. Deterrence (Strategy).   4. Strategic
Defense Initiative.   5. Statesmen—United States—
Interviews.   I. Star wars history.   II. Title.
UA23.C516   1987   355'.0335'73   87-8583
ISBN 0-674-32346-7
ISBN 0-674-32347- 5 (pbk.)

CONTENTS

★ ★

INTRODUCTION

THE CONTRIBUTORS TO THIS oral history are, first and foremost, eminent Americans (including a former President) who have made or helped to make crucial decisions concerning the role of nuclear weapons. These major decisions of our nuclear era, given by their orders or maintained under their immediate inspection, have created the architecture of nuclear deterrence upon which civilisation's survival has been staked – deterrence rather than defence. It is from this point, beginning with a great debate of more than a quarter of a century ago, that we should explore the source and follow the path to President Reagan's 'Star Wars' – which is strategic *defence* – as history.

Although 'Star Wars' is still experiments and distant hopes, and so resists definition in terms of either programme or policy, the notion of strategic defence involves ultimately a rejection of deterrence as we have known it. At the Icelandic summit in the autumn of 1986, where Mr Gorbachev and President Reagan reached an impasse over arms control on the Strategic Defence Initiative issue, the two leaders appear to have agreed to the elimination of all ballistic missiles – this to be achieved in a decade. While there has been some retreat since from that startling proposal, it cannot be dismissed from the historical record. The SDI, it seemed, had already set in motion a revolution in perceptions.

Like Gibbon's description of the virtue of Marcus Aurelius, the evolution of the American strategic debate has been 'the well-earned harvest of many a learned conference, of many a patient lecture, and many a midnight lucubration'. But our contributors to this 'Star Wars' history are men to whom it fell, in the end, actually to *decide*. They are also men whose task was to give advice, and whose advice, therefore, directly influenced those decisions. It is the design of this oral history to explore with these decision-makers the nature of their patience – and their exasperation. In the following pages, and in their own words, they give their reasons.

The interviews were recorded in the spring and summer of 1985 in the United States and Europe. What each contributor has to say is what was recorded on the spot, at the time. No subsequent alterations have been made, except in instances where the conventions of the spoken word in print may have left meaning in doubt. Those taking part were informed in advance of the areas of my questions, to enable them where possible to consult diaries or official documents; thereafter, the interviews took the form of a 'live' conversation, recorded at a single sitting.

The 'Star Wars' history was commissioned by the Talks and Documentaries Department of BBC Radio and broadcast originally as six programmes by Radio 3. It has been possible to include more material and more contributors' voices in this book than the generous constraints of broadcasting time on Radio 3 allowed. This first-hand evidence of the American strategic debate continues the activity of oral history inaugurated by BBC Talks and Documentaries (Radio) which has, so far, included 'Many Reasons Why', on the American involvement in Vietnam; 'The Price of Victory', the history of Britain's European diplomacy up to the time of General de Gaulle's 'veto' of Britain's first attempt to join the European Community; and 'The Eagle and the Small Birds', subtitled Crisis in the Soviet Empire: from Yalta to Solidarity. All three have also been expanded and published in book form by BBC Publications.

My gratitude is due on several counts. First, to the many distinguished contributors who have given generously to the BBC both their time and personal recollections of the severe and exacting history of the nuclear experience. In particular is it due to George Fischer, Head of Talks and Documentaries at Broadcasting House, and to Ian McIntyre, Controller of Radio 3, for their stimulation and active support of endeavours such as these. And finally to my colleague Anne Winder, who produced the original broadcasts for Radio 3 in 1985, and whose organisational skills successfully 'gathered all the waters together unto one place' – or rather, within a short time, in different cities and different countries.

Michael Charlton
Broadcasting House, London
March 1987

★ 1 ★
DISILLUSION WITH DEFENCE:

The Mortification of Robert McNamara

FOR THE FIRST time since Hiroshima and Nagasaki were destroyed by the sun of Los Alamos, the possibility of *defence* against nuclear bombardment is being taken seriously. If successful it would mean a radical transformation of the competition between the two contending political wills of the Soviet Union and the Western Alliance.

If strategic defence were also to become a Russian achievement, it would place a question mark against the present forces and philosophy of the smaller nuclear powers (China, France and Britain), who would have to think all over again. The mercurial Americans are poised for another advance. With that prospect, a gap in strategic capabilities – so far unique in history – appears to be opening between the United States and Western Europe, a gap at present bridged by the national nuclear deterrents of Britain and France. Is President Reagan's vision that the ballistic missile might be made 'impotent' and 'obsolete' evidence only of the intellectual pathos of our time – the longing to escape from an intolerable yet permanent dilemma? It has already become part of the historic dialogue of our day.

In the 1960s, the Americans arrived at an opposite conclusion. They took the view that *defence* against the ballistic missile should be all but abandoned. This American insight and initiative led to the Anti-Ballistic Missile Treaty, the centre-piece of the first arms control agreements with the Soviet Union. Nuclear realities, it was supposed, had forced potential enemies to reach agreement and had imposed upon them a common sobriety and moderation.

The purpose of this 'Star Wars' history is to review the intervening years and follow the evolution of this American debate with those, including a former President, who have shaped and made the crucial decisions; and to ask how it is that – having forsaken defence and accepted the threat of 'mutual annihilation' as the basis for stable conflict and rivalry with the

Soviet Union – disillusion with arms control took root. Why, now, do the Americans believe the time has come to reconsider the stand they took two decades ago, and to pursue an alternative to 'mutual assured destruction' and its stark acronym, MAD?

Few public men have influenced the way we think about nuclear weapons more than Robert McNamara, Defence Secretary to Presidents John Kennedy and Lyndon Johnson. What one might call the mortification of Robert McNamara was the act of self-denial and subjection of American appetite which he sponsored in relinquishing the idea of defending populations against the Bomb. Mr McNamara recalls the inner Cabinet meeting which laid the foundation for the publicly declared strategic architecture with which we live today.

ROBERT MCNAMARA: In November 1966, Cyrus Vance and I (Cy was then my deputy Secretary for Defence), Walt Rostow (the National Security Adviser), with the five Chiefs of Staff went to Texas to meet with President Johnson, who was then in Austin. The purpose of the meeting was to review the military budget which we would submit to the Congress in January of 1967 to cover the fiscal year 1968. A major issue was the issue of anti-ballistic missile defence. The Congress at that point had already authorised procurement of an anti-ballistic missile defence and appropriated funds for it. We had refused to spend the funds – even in the face of the fact that the Soviets were then deploying an anti-ballistic missile defence around Moscow. When we came to that part of the budget I remember very well that the five Chiefs unanimously recommended to the President that we include in our budget proposal for the Congress funds for the production and deployment of an anti-ballistic missile defence. The President turned to me and asked me what my recommendation was. I said, 'Mr President, that's absolutely wrong. I strongly recommend against it.'

He turned to Walt Rostow. Walt joined with the Chiefs. He turned to Cy. Cy said, 'I strongly agree with Bob.' So we had a situation where the five Chiefs of Staff and the nation's security adviser were taking one decision and the Secretary of Defence and his Deputy were taking another. That's a miserable position for a President. I did not like to push him too hard under those circumstances.

I said to him, 'Mr President, let's do this. Let's recognise that I think it's irrational to react to the Soviet defence with a US defence – it will be ineffective and a waste of money. But let's put the funds in the budget proposal and state to the Congress that none of this money will be utilised until we have made an effort to join with the Soviets to negotiate an agreement (a) to limit, and hopefully terminate, any anti-ballistic missile defence, and (b) with that as a foundation to move ahead on limiting future *offensive* weapons deployments.'

He said, 'I accept that.' That began the contacts with the Soviet Union which ultimately led to the ABM Treaty in 1972 and the Offensive Arms Protocol that accompanied it.

CHARLTON: But by that time you had reached a position in your own mind where 'mutual assured destruction' was the only conceivable way to live with the advent of the nuclear weapon?

McNAMARA: That is correct.

CHARLTON: And, because you assumed that the Soviet Union would subscribe to MAD, this was to be the basis of (1) a stable deterrence, and (2) arms control?

McNAMARA: I didn't assume the Soviets subscribed to it. The way they were behaving on ballistic missile defence cast some doubt on it. But we believed that, ultimately, through the negotiations we would reach a common agreement on that as the foundation; and that would then make possible offensive arms limitation.

CHARLTON: What I was going to put to you, though, is this: isn't a shared perception of doctrine more or less essential to the pursuit of arms control?

McNAMARA: Absolutely – and what I assumed was that while they might not *at that moment* subscribe to that doctrine, the negotiations themselves would lead to acceptance of a common doctrine, on the basis of which one then could build arms control agreements.

ROBERT McNAMARA leaves us with one of the unknowns, unresolved today and still an issue: whether the acceptance of a common vulnerability could be based, with confidence, on a reasonable common understanding. After all, the opinions of the democrat are deemed by the Marxist-Leninist to be ideological fictions. The perception that animated the Americans then was their unilateral conclusion that the means of defence could compromise stability as much as the means of attack. It is an argument deployed now against the 'Star Wars' concept. Dean Rusk was Secretary of State to both Presidents Kennedy and Johnson.

DEAN RUSK: We did a great deal of work on the anti-ballistic missile problem in 1965 and 1966. We came to the conclusion that if we and the Soviets began to deploy anti-ballistic missiles, the inevitable result would be a dramatic increase in *offensive* missiles, so that you could penetrate or saturate the ABMs before the main strike was delivered. Secretary McNamara had gone through that very careful analysis in 1966. He seemed to me to be able to demonstrate conclusively that the primary result of ABMs would be to multiply *offensive* weapons, and that therefore they didn't make any sense. They would simply result in a severe escalation of the race in offensive weapons. That underlying consideration produced the Anti-Ballistic Missile Treaty.

AS THE SOVIET NUCLEAR ARSENAL was growing reciprocally in the 1960s, the opinion had clearly matured among those who had direct

responsibility for these matters in the United States that nuclear blackmail
– the use of the nuclear threat with any *positive* goal in mind – could
occupy no place in the thinking of the statesman. We can assume that the
existence of these monstrous weapons weighs heavily.

DEAN RUSK: Oh yes! I remember almost immediately after President
Kennedy took office, he and about six of us sat down in the Cabinet Room.
We spent most of the day going through the total effects of nuclear war,
both direct and indirect. At the end of it he asked me to come back to the
Oval Office with him to talk about something. As we went through the
door he said, with a strange little look on his face, 'And we call ourselves
the human race . . .' Those who go through that exercise know that at long
last the human race has reached the point where it must prevent that
general war before it occurs. It is going to take some doing in terms of
imagination and restraint and responsibility, and I personally think we
need more help from the Russians on that kind of thing than we have had.
CHARLTON: Why, therefore, do you suppose Khruschev tried diplomacy
by nuclear intimidation in the 1960s?
RUSK: I was with President Kennedy at the Summit meeting in Vienna in
June 1961. It became clear before the end of the meeting that Mr
Khruschev was trying to intimidate this new, young President of the
United States through the ultimatum on Berlin – which was delivered in a
pretty bald and ruthless fashion. At one point Khruschev said to Kennedy,
'Now this is what we are going to do in Berlin. If there is any interference
from the West – there will be war.'

In diplomacy you do not use the word war. You talk about 'gravest
possible consequences', or something of that sort. But Kennedy had to
look him straight in the eye and say, 'Then Mr Chairman, there is going to
be a war. It is going to be a very cold winter.'

I don't know why Khruschev undertook that particular pressure on
Kennedy in those circumstances, but it did cause President Kennedy to
realise that here was a man who had to be faced up to, and curbed, or we
could have some major problems. I think Mr Khruschev would have been
glad to pick up any pieces he could along the way – by pressure and threats.

DEAN RUSK'S DISAPPROVAL of the withholding by the Russians of
co-operation 'in terms of imagination and restraint and responsibility'
identifies the source of a persistent mistrust. Do the two sides arm
themselves for different purposes? Can equality ever be conceded or
established? The uncertainties which arise are translated into profound
political consequences. The suspicions engendered recall Metternich's
famous remark in the last century when he was informed of the death of
the Russian Ambassador. 'Is this true?' he asked, adding, 'What can have
been his motive?'

In the 1960s, American policy makers were absorbing the shock of the

Soviet Union being the first to produce an intercontinental ballistic missile – and the exuberant claims made by Khruschev which accompanied Moscow's success. The American homeland was, henceforth, no longer an invulnerable sanctuary. In addition, the Russians had shown that they were capable of surreptitiously gaining an unpredicted strategic advantage. Sputnik evoked fearful prospects of Soviet-imposed 'Munichs' and 'Pearl Harbours'.

President Kennedy had campaigned on the issue of America 'asleep' and 'falling behind'. Only later (with satellite reconnaissance) could it be shown that the 'missile gap' – the fear that the Soviet Union might produce intercontinental rockets and put them into the field faster than the United States – was illusory. However, this began an intelligence debate which continues to the present day: would the Soviet Union ever be content with parity?

ROBERT MCNAMARA: The first action I took as Secretary of Defence was to determine the size of that gap and how we should react to it – what additional forces we should put in place to offset this alleged advantage of the Soviet Union. We learned that while there was a gap, it was a gap that favoured the United States and not the Soviet Union. Now, President Kennedy did not conceive of this gap himself. He was not consciously misstating the situation as he knew it. It turned out that there were *two* intelligence estimates in the US government. One was prepared by the Air Force and the other by the Central Intelligence Agency. The Air Force estimate was the basis for the allegation that the Soviet strength substantially exceeded that of the United States. Again, I want to stress that the Air Force was not consciously misleading the recipients of its reports. The problem then, and to a considerable degree today, is that the West has imperfect knowledge of the Soviet Union, and when you face a situation of imperfect knowledge, it's very important that you do not underestimate the strength of your opponent. You tend to overestimate. That's what the Air Force was doing then, and that led to the allegation of the 'missile gap'. To this day, in my opinion, we're exaggerating the strength of the Soviets for the same reason.

CHARLTON: Given a disposition by some to suppose that 'bomber gaps' and 'missile gaps' are to be attributed to villainy on the part of statesmen, isn't the problem inseparable from the Soviet Union as a closed and secretive society?

MCNAMARA: Yes, and I would like to stress that I think it is in the Soviet interest to open that up to some degree, at least – to share with us, and permit us to understand better what their security policies and their security forces are. It would be very much in their interest, for example, to allow us to verify some of the actions under the treaties. At the present time the US Administration sincerely and strongly believes that the Soviets are following a policy of violating the Anti-Ballistic Missile and Arms

Limitation Treaties. In the Soviet's own interests, they should open up and allow us to determine whether that is true.

CHARLTON: But, after the launching of Sputnik, would you agree that Khruschev brandished the nuclear weapon and the Soviet Union's nuclear success? I have here an extract from his speech of 14 June 1960:

> The United States, for example, has set itself the target of equalling Soviet rocket production within a period of five years. Do you think the Russians are going to wait? Are we going to play tiddly-winks? Naturally we shall try to make the most of our time lead and do everything to retain our leading position in this field. There has been a fundamental change in the balance of strength between the Capitalist and Socialist countries – the old position-of-strength policy is no longer tenable . . .

How did the Kennedy Administration tend to react in the face of those pronouncements?

MCNAMARA: You must recall that, at that time, the Soviets knew their weakness, probably better than we did. The number of strategic warheads possessed by the Soviet Union and the US in 1960, I happen to recall – I was reviewing the figures the other day – the US had 6300, the Soviets had 200. Now, facing that situation and recognising as he did that there were individuals high in the hierarchy in the Defence Department who believed that we did have, should have, and possibly should use a first-strike capability, I think it was natural that Khruschev would tend to exaggerate their strength and boast of what they were going to do to us – recognising that we did not know exactly what they had, and recognising that they had for a short period of time a technological lead (that is to say in rocket, in missile development). I think that accounts for what clearly was a gross exaggeration of strength.

CHARLTON: But we should be clear that that is with the benefit of hindsight, and not what you knew at the time.

MCNAMARA: Yes, that's exactly the point.

THE SOVIET UNION HAD neutralised the major Western advantage, and nuclear weapons were serving as the agents of mutual paralysis at the level of grand strategy. As Kennedy had concluded in 1960:

> Soviet missile power will be the shield from behind which they will slowly but surely advance, through Sputnik diplomacy, limited wars, and the vicious blackmail of our allies. The periphery of the free world will be nibbled away.

The inference was that nuclear weapons favoured the aggressor and that the Soviet Union was an aggressive state. In this respect opinion was influenced by the experience of the immediate historical past, as Dean Rusk makes clear.

DEAN RUSK: That continuing build-up is a matter of concern. Let me go back here for a bit. Just after the end of World War II, we in the West demobilised almost completely and almost overnight. By the summer of 1946, we did not have a single division in our Army nor a single group in our Air Force that could be considered ready for combat. The ships of our

Navy were being put into mothballs about as fast as we could find berths for them, and those that remained afloat were being manned by skeleton crews. Our defence budget for three fiscal years, 1947, 1948 and 1949, came down to eleven billion dollars a year, believe it or not.

Now Mr Stalin sat over there, and he looked out across the West, and he saw all the divisions melting away. So what did he do? He tried to keep his troops in Azerbaijan, the north-west province of Iran – the first case before the UN Security Council. He demanded the two eastern provinces of Turkey, Kars and Ardahan. He swept aside some of the wartime agreements which might have given the peoples of Eastern Europe more say in their own political future. He supported the guerrillas going after Greece. He had a hand in the Communist *coup d'état* in Czechoslovakia. He blockaded Berlin. He gave the green light to the North Koreans to go after South Korea.

Now this was at a period when we were disarmed. I personally believe that we in the West exposed Mr Stalin to intolerable temptations through our own weakness. But those adventures of his, just after World War II, were the origins of the Cold War. We were disarmed. Had he pursued for ten years after World War II a policy of *genuine* peaceful co-existence, as we in the West would understand it, he would have produced among other things a disarmed and isolationist America. But he woke us up with all those adventures of his.

THOSE WHO MADE AMERICAN policy in the 1960s were confronted with a reality beyond the range of all former concepts: the principle of 'mutual annihilation' was becoming a material fact. Robert McNamara, who had 'industrialised' the military arts – and in doing so quickly overhauled and then outdistanced the early Soviet supremacy in ballistic rockets – had begun his personal odyssey to the meeting he would have some years later with the Soviet Premier Alexei Kosygin. In Glassboro, New Jersey, in 1967, the Defence Secretary made a passionate plea to the Russians to forgo the concept of defence against the ballistic missile. During these dramatic years (spanning the crises over Berlin and Cuba to the time when the American commitment to Vietnam was at its zenith), Robert McNamara tried to reconcile old concepts with the new realities of approaching nuclear parity.

ROBERT McNAMARA: I remember being with President Kennedy in May of 1962, in California. We were visiting Vandenberg Air Force Base, and the Commander of the Strategic Air Command met us when our plane landed. As we got into his car, he turned to the President and said, 'When we get the 10,000 Minutemen, Mr President, I . . .'

At that moment the President said, 'What did you say?'

'Well, I started to say when we get the 10,000 Minutemen, we're going to do . . .'

The President said, 'I *thought* that's what you said.' And he turned to me and said, 'Bob, we're not going to get 10,000 Minutemen, are we?'

I said, 'No, Mr President, we're limiting it to 1000.'

The reason I mention this is that at that point the Commander of the Strategic Air Command believed we should have 10,000. The Air Force had cut that back and, as I recall, had recommended to me that we procure 3000. I had cut it back to 1000. Now I think one could argue that 1000 was too many. And that's about as far as I thought I could go in the circumstances.

CHARLTON: You've said a good deal in the past about 'the cycle of action and reaction'. In September 1967 you made a speech in San Francisco in which you spoke of your certainty that action and reaction fuelled the arms race. I'd like to quote your words to you:

> There's a kind of mad momentum intrinsic to the development of all nuclear weapons. If a weapons system works, and works well, there's strong pressure from many directions to procure and deploy the system out of all proportion to the prudent level required.

I'd like to ask if that is not too mechanical an explanation. Doesn't it ignore the ideological conflict and doctrinal contention which exist between the two powers?

MCNAMARA: I think it is the ideological differences that in effect cause the action-reaction phenomenon in the technology of weapons – given each side's fear of the other. When one side sees the other side moving forward technically, they're driven to a technical response. Therefore I think my statement is entirely consistent with your implication that ideological differences exist.

CHARLTON: The only question is, which would you put first?

MCNAMARA: I wouldn't put either first. They exist together in the world today. Ideological differences persist; each side is fearful of the other; technology advances. If one side introduces a technical advance, the other side is driven to copy it. I think we have a perfect illustration of that today and I'm not sure either side fully recognises it. President Reagan's 'Star Wars' initiative is bound to lead, in my opinion, to Soviet responses. There's very little evidence that the US Administration has yet taken account of these responses.

CHARLTON: Responses in kind, or of a different kind?

MCNAMARA: I would say both, in kind in the sense that our expansion of research on strategic defences is bound to lead to further Soviet effort in that direction. Moreover, our stated intention to *deploy* strategic defence will almost surely lead, unless we backtrack, to an expansion of Soviet offensive forces, in order that they will have continuing confidence in their ability to deter a strike by us.

CHARLTON: How similar are these arguments to the ones you had with Kosygin at Glassboro?

MCNAMARA: They are the mirror image of the positions in 1967. The positions have exactly reversed.

CHARLTON: But are the arguments not changed, or the emphasis in the arguments changed, because the technology today is different?

McNAMARA: They have changed in one sense, and it is a very important sense. Let me digress to explain something which I think is not well understood in the US and may not be well understood in Europe. There are *two* 'Star Wars' programmes. There is what I call 'Star Wars I', which is President Reagan's proposal in his speech of 23 March 1983 – that is to say, a 'leak-proof' defence which, he stated, would permit the destruction of offensive weapons and the replacement of those *offensive* weapons by *defensive* weapons. Now, I do not know any reputable scientist in this country today who believes that a 'leak-proof' defensive system will prove technically feasible any time within the next several decades, and save the lives of our children and grandchildren. However, President Reagan continues to pursue that objective. All others I would say (with the possible exception of Secretary Weinberger) who are supporting strategic defence, and there are many – scientists, arms control experts and military leaders in the US – are supporting what I call 'Star Wars II'. Now that is a *partial* defence. It could range all the way from a defence of our missile sites, to command centres, to a partial defence of populations. But 'Star Wars II' defences will be *added* to offensive systems, not *replace* them. In a little-remembered sentence of that same 23 March 1983 speech, after the President had said that his objective for the scientists was to develop a 'leak-proof' defence, he went on to say that if, instead of replacing the offensive systems with defensive systems, we *add* the defensive system to the offensive, the Soviets will consider this aggressive and 'no one wants that'. That, however, is what 'Star Wars II' is designed to do. That is exactly the way the Soviets are interpreting it, and that is a very great danger.

CHARLTON: At a recent seminar held by ex-President Carter in Atlanta, attended by Soviet representatives and many former American Cabinet ministers from several administrations, the Soviet Ambassador Dobrynin made use of a homely analogy from American football. He said it was rather like the Washington Redskins and the Miami Cowboys (*sic*). (Clearly he thought the Redskins were the Soviet side and, I suppose, the Miami Cowboys were a reference to the United States.) 'What did they expect the Redskins to do', Dobrynin said, 'if the Miami Cowboys deployed a brand new defence? Of course, the Redskins would follow suit . . .'

Do you accept the logic of that?

McNAMARA: Absolutely. You just think of Dobrynin as McNamara and Reagan as Kosygin in 1967. You have exactly the same language.

ONE LEGACY OF THE McNamara years was that America stopped building ballistic missiles in the 1960s and kept to an overall level which stayed the same until 1980. The Russians' refusal to halt when they reached the same level has nourished the suspicion that the official ideology of the Soviet Union imposes and sustains a rather different view of the nuclear weapon. In the strange universe called into existence by weapons which have no function except to stop themselves being used, and which can only discharge that function because there is a chance that they might be, is it the case that the Soviet Union also believes that nuclear arms inaugurated a strategy of deterrence? That deterrence has been substituted for decision as the fundamental objective of war? General William Odom, former Assistant Chief of Staff for Intelligence and an influential adviser on Soviet policy in the Pentagon, is now Director of the National Security Agency.

GENERAL WILLIAM ODOM: I don't think the Soviets accept that at all. The classified studies (most of them are declassified now) don't demonstrate that at all; they demonstrate quite the contrary. I have gone back and looked at some of the evidence. It may be that Khruschev looked at heavy reliance on strategic nuclear weapons as a way to get around building very large ground forces, particularly *paying* for the modernisation of ground forces and weapons.

CHARLTON: Rather like we've done in the West?

ODOM: Yes.

CHARLTON: But when it comes to policy making in the United States, to what extent are you people in intelligence persuaded that the Soviet Union has formed views about the political and military usefulness of nuclear weapons which differ significantly from the views we hold about them in the West?

ODOM: There has always been a small number of people in the intelligence community and in the policy community who were sceptical about the symmetry of doctrinal views. By the late 1970s, evidence was beginning to accumulate in the form of weapons systems: for example, missile silos that could be reloaded. With our doctrine you don't need a silo that can be reloaded, because you don't expect to shoot. When we began to see reload capacities in the Soviet case, it raised the question – why? It suggests that one expects to be firing missiles later on – maybe two, three, four? Who knows how many? We saw a number of other force-structure developments that suggested strongly that Soviet employment doctrine for these would not be the same as our doctrine at all. I think our view began to shift in official documents under the Carter Administration. Now, under the Reagan Administration, I think the dominant view is that there are rather significant asymmetries between the Soviet view of how they would employ their weapon systems and how the United States, the West, would expect strategic forces, in particular, to be used.

CHARLTON: How did Marxist-Leninist ideology accommodate this transcendent new fact of nuclear weapons?

ODOM: I don't think that Stalin was as 'buffaloed' by it as Khruschev was. He did not allow himself to get into the trap of being vulnerable to the charge which the Chinese levelled at the Russians in the 1960s. Khruschev began to make noises to the effect that 'War is no longer inevitable' because of the destructive nature of nuclear weapons – echoing certain things that were being said in the West. The Chinese promptly turned round and said, 'If that's true, it means that material and technical factors of war now have primacy over policy.' Lenin always argued that *policy* had primacy over these other things, as long as you took a scientific Marxist view of the interaction of those material forces. How could this be? Stalin never lent himself to that charge. In fact, he was publicly very quiet on the issue, which has led many people in the West to misjudge the evolution of Soviet views on nuclear weapons from 1945 to 1953.

CHARLTON: Stalin made one remark about nuclear weapons (at that time it was the atomic weapon and before the thermonuclear bombs) which I imagine many people recall. He said, 'Nuclear weapons frighten people with weak nerves.' Are you saying that his rather cynical, *Realpolitik* appraisal underlies Soviet policy, or was that supplanted by the advent of hydrogen bombs of infinitely greater destructive power than anything dropped at Hiroshima or Nagasaki?

ODOM: That remark, which Stalin made to Milovan Djilas shortly after the War, may indeed reflect the finite limits of atomic weapons as opposed to the larger finite limits of fusion bombs. Nonetheless, in that somewhat visceral psychological observation of Stalin's there is, I think, a real insight into the Soviet reaction and approach to nuclear weapons.

CHARLTON: But experts point out that you can search Soviet military writing and find there no analogue for this Western concept of deterrence. Do you agree with that?

ODOM: I agree with that completely. We had an American political scientist, Graham Allison, who argued that there were three models of decision making: a rational model, an organisational model, and a bureaucratic model. His organisational model rested on the assumption that you can do what you are *organised* to do. If you are *not* organised to do a particular thing, then it is very unlikely that a government can exercise that choice. I think that is a terribly relevant insight for military affairs. If the Soviet Union is organised to use their nuclear weapons the way we do, then they've got that option. If they're *not* organised to use them in that way and they're organised to use them in some other way, then they're going to do what they've designed and trained to do. I find the best evidence for inferring what the Soviets are most likely to do in their doctrinal literature. This creates a bibliography of textbooks which Soviet officers have to study, which becomes the basis for their education and their views about how these weapons will be employed. After a war starts, to try to change everybody's doctrinal view about such employment – that's virtually incomprehensible. Therefore, one or two isolated statements by Khruschev or Brezhnev strike me as very thin evidence indeed about the Soviet view of nuclear weapons or approach to their use.

These textbooks are studied and memorised in great detail. When you stack that against the empirical evidence we see in their force-building process, it leads me to the very comfortable conclusion – or maybe uncomfortable, but confident conclusion – that they don't share our view of that at all.

CHARLTON: So there are these publicly formulated positions, including what were once classified studies, but do you feel convinced that there is a private view in the Kremlin which differs from that? Or do you assume that your 'worst possible case' is also that privately held view?

ODOM: I can never know precisely what view a person in the Kremlin holds.

CHARLTON: I thought that's what your job was.

ODOM: The only way I know you can get that view is to poll them. I would love to conduct a poll, if I were permitted to do so! I consider that a very difficult research task, one that I'm not going to waste a great deal of time on because I don't see much prospect of success.

CHARLTON: What is the distinction they make, then, between deterrence and war, in the sense that Clausewitz saw war as the 'continuation of politics by other means'?

ODOM: He saw war as an instrument of policy. Clausewitz is much quoted and little read – there are many other things by Clausewitz which you could bring to bear, and I think the Soviets are somewhat better students of Clausewitz than we sometimes are in the West. You know, Lenin himself read Clausewitz very carefully and annotated *On War* in some detail. I think he is very close to the Soviet view of war. In fact, I would like to point out that there was a Clausewitzian triad. There was the notion of 'nation' which gives the passion for war; the General Staff and the Cabinet which are the rational, guiding system for war; and then, the uncertainties of the battlefield before the war. Lenin could very easily substitute the Party and the General Staff for the Cabinet and the General Staff. He could assert 'class' for 'nation'. And he was very pragmatic about the uncertainties of the battlefield, both political and military. Therefore the Clausewitzian paradigm of war fits very neatly into his thought about these things.

In addition to Clausewitz, there is an ideological point that seems to me to bear very heavily on the side of those who argue that the Soviets take a war-fighting approach. To take the Western deterrence view of 'assured destruction' is really to say that we surrender primacy over our choice about matters of war to technical gimmickry. In other words, we determine the outcomes in advance, and just sit back and let somebody else make the choice about whether deterrence will fail or not. There are so many paradoxes (philosophical, moral, military and others) in deterrence theory, it's amazing that this paradigm has succeeded as long as it has. From time to time I have described it as Ptolemy's view of the solar system. When the stars don't behave the way you want them to, you create one more little epicycle to account for this erratic behaviour by the Soviets. I think the Soviets have a Copernican view of the solar system.

CHARLTON: In other words, you are saying that your assessment in the

Pentagon is that the Soviet Union refuses to adopt this doctrine of 'assured destruction' because it thinks – ideologically and empirically – that you cannot, just because nuclear weapons exist, rob war of any strategic meaning. In other words, you've got to keep on *thinking* – if deterrence fails.

ODOM: Precisely. I would call deterrence, when it's based on an empty threat (from a Marxist-Leninist point of view), an error of subjectivism. In other words, you don't have the objective material factors to make it come out the way you've asserted it will come out. Our deterrence theory would strike a Soviet, a serious Marxist-Leninist, as simple-minded subjectivism, or bourgeois idealism, whereas an objective war-fighting capability that has the prospect of some campaign success, even at great losses to your own society, is an *objective* capability, not simply a subjective capability.

THE PRIVATE VIEW IN the Kremlin of these vital matters remains inaccessible, as both Robert McNamara and Dean Rusk have complained. In such circumstances, it was the Duke of Wellington who advised us that the business of war and the business of life was to find out what you don't know from what you do and to *guess* what was at the other side of the hill. How, therefore, do we suppose that the Soviet Union views the political and military utility of nuclear weapons? A family descendant of the great Duke, who has held high responsibility for the conduct of Alliance nuclear policy, is Field Marshal Lord Carver.

LORD CARVER: I think that the principal political utility is to reinforce their claim to be a world power on the same level as the United States. This is very deeply ingrained in their thinking: politically, they must be seen (partly in order to be seen as the leaders of world Communism) as in every way the equals of the United States.

CHARLTON: But would you agree that the extent to which the Soviet approach to the problem of nuclear weapons differs from the Alliance or American ones has been the crux of recent debate? What is the evidence that the Russians feel the nuclear weapon has abolished what has historically been an indispensable concept of war – decisive battle? In other words, that they, too, have substituted deterrence for decisive battle?

CARVER: I don't think that is the case at all, certainly not in the eyes of the Soviet military. I think they initially saw (as, in many ways, we did, too) the nuclear weapon, the atom bomb as we called it in those days, as an extension of fire-power on the battlefield. We have looked at it in terms of an extension of fire-power *defensively*; they had looked at it as an extension of fire-power *offensively*. Their whole strategic doctrine is based on their absolute determination not (as they see it) to make the same mistake they made in 1941, of remaining on the defensive. The moment they feel or suspect that the other side is about to take military operations against them, they must take the offensive and be capable of winning that offensive in as short a time as possible. Therefore, their whole strategic doctrine (which they regard as being for the purposes of defence) is one of being able to take the *offence*; and for that they have to have what they call 'the correct correlation of forces', which means that they've got to be superior to the other side.

CHARLTON: What they call a correlation of forces, a 'balance', to them is an imbalance in their favour?

CARVER: That is exactly the case.

CHARLTON: Their publicly articulated position over many years has been 'no first use' of nuclear weapons. In what circumstances do you believe that the Soviet Union *would* go first with nuclear weapons?

CARVER: Well, I tackled them on this particular issue, particularly in respect of the SS–20. I said, 'You made a declaration of "no first use" – but land-based missile systems which are designed to attack the other side's nuclear delivery systems, whether they're mobile or static, are by definition first-use weapons because there's absolutely no point in firing at the other side's nuclear delivery system after it's already fired! So how,' I said, 'do you explain that away?'

And they said, 'Ah, but you see, as long as the United States won't make such a declaration, we must assume (and they do in their minds assume) '. . . that the United States is planning a first strike against us. And we must, therefore, make provision for the fact that this is the case, and when we come to the conclusion that they are about to carry out that operation, we would strike their systems first.' In other words, they *would* carry out a *first* strike. Of course, it's a mirror image of what the United States themselves think.

CHARLTON: However, President Nixon is on the record as saying this:

> For years the prevailing United States concept has been that nuclear war could not and would not bring about any meaningful form of victory, either military or political. The Soviet concept, however, has been that nuclear war, even though it would mean an immense disaster, cannot and must not be deprived of strategic meaning.

What is the strategic meaning that the Soviet Union would give to it?

CARVER: I think it is this. Certainly the Soviet military, as I see it, take the view that they don't want a nuclear war any more than anybody else. But if a war starts and nuclear weapons are used, there can be no limitation; and there *would* be no limitation from their point of view in how their nuclear weapons were used. If the worst came to the worst, they are prepared to face all-out nuclear war in the belief that the Soviet system (as well as the geography of the Soviet Union) is one which would survive such an exchange better than the Western system.

IT IS AT THIS LAST and crucial point – envisaging the fighting and winning of nuclear war – that there is a clear separation between the maintained Soviet view and that which Robert McNamara came to hold and implement as the public nuclear doctrine of the United States and its allies in the 1960s: 'mutual assured destruction'. As Defence Secretary,

McNamara had been the prophet of record for two schools of thought – first providing the American President with the option of first use of nuclear weapons against Soviet military forces (the 'counterforce strategy') and then, as the Soviet arsenal grew, deciding that such 'positive' use of nuclear weapons could really only belong to the realms of strategic fiction. He describes how this doctrine, applied to the fantastic destructive power of nuclear weapons, evolved in his own mind during the 1960s.

ROBERT McNAMARA: First we quickly came to the conclusion that 'massive retaliation', which had been the officially accepted strategy of NATO, was no longer tenable. We must move away from it. It was inconceivable that we would respond to even small forms of conventional aggression by the Soviets in Western Europe with a US strike on Moscow – which was the essence of the doctrine of 'massive retaliation'. Why did we come to that conclusion? Because it became very clear that, were we to respond to a small conventional attack in Western Europe by striking Moscow with a nuclear weapon – the next day, or that same day, the Soviets would attack New York or London or Paris or Washington, and with such destruction that we would never make the first move. It would be committing suicide.

CHARLTON: This is the dilemma of 'extended' deterrence for the United States?

McNAMARA: It is indeed. We recommended 'flexible response', which has an element of extended deterrence in it. But we considered that the extended deterrent element – that is, using nuclear weapons in response to Soviet conventional attack – was a last resort action. We urged that NATO reduce substantially the likelihood that it would ever be required, by increasing *conventional* forces. (I hasten to add here that the proposal was very controversial. It took five years for NATO to adopt it. When it did adopt it, in 1967, it didn't do so in its entirety. To this day, the NATO strategy depends on early response to Soviet conventional attack by utilising nuclear weapons.) As I say, we were seeking to move away from 'massive retaliation', to replace it (a) with conventional response to conventional attack, and (b) to the extent that nuclear weapons were to be used, to use them late and in limited quantity, and against military as opposed to population targets, in order to limit the Soviet nuclear response and thereby limit the damage to NATO.

CHARLTON: There is a doctrinal shift during what are known as 'the McNamara years', away from the idea that the prime target should be Soviet military forces and back to the idea that the populations of both countries should be 'held hostage' . . .

McNAMARA: A shift to 'assured destruction'.

CHARLTON: To 'assured destruction'. Now, was that a unilateral choice by you?

McNAMARA: Yes. 'Unilateral choice' in this sense. The Soviet forces increased in size. In 1960, I think the number of their strategic warheads was 200, and by 1970 that had risen to 1800. During that time, the number of their missiles had been increased. It became increasingly clear that a second strike against their missiles (in other words, a retaliatory counterforce strike) made no sense. The Soviet missiles were very likely to have been fired by the time our counterforce got there.

CHARLTON: You'd be firing at empty holes . . .

McNAMARA: Firing at empty holes. The counterforce strategy was a function of a very limited Soviet strategic nuclear capability. It was appropriate for 1962. By 1964–66, it was no longer appropriate, as they had multiplied their strategic nuclear capability several-fold.

CHARLTON: As you settled into the Kennedy Administration, could you say, with Clausewitz, that you were 'a man of action with all your soul', and that you wanted 'to think out, with all your soul, your own activity and your action in general'? How did you contemplate this whole question of equality and superiority as between the Soviet Communist Republic and the American Republic?

McNAMARA: You're quite right, we did want to think it out, and particularly we wanted to think it out because we recognised that, without exaggeration, the very existence of our society and civilisation was at stake. That reality was forced upon us very quickly. You may remember that in August of 1961, a few months after the Kennedy Administration took office, the Soviets began to put pressure on West Berlin, clearly with the intention of changing the agreements and in a very real sense taking over the Western position in West Berlin. We then had to consider how to respond; and in the course of a period of time that extended over several weeks, we examined possible responses – including, at the suggestion of some senior commanders, the possible use of nuclear weapons. Beginning then, and extending months into the future, we studied intensively how, if at all, NATO might initiate the use of nuclear weapons with advantage to NATO. I did not find then, and I've never seen since, any indication that anyone in the world knows how to initiate the use of nuclear weapons with advantage to NATO. At that point we came to the conclusion that nuclear warheads are not weapons; they have no military value whatsoever, excepting only to serve as a deterrent to one's opponent's use of such weapons.

CHARLTON: But the Kennedy Administration had set out to re-establish a superiority America had enjoyed since the nuclear age began, and which the Russians had challenged by being first with an intercontinental ballistic missile. Did you subscribe to the notion that the nuclear weapon had made 'absolute war' impossible?

McNAMARA: No, I don't want to say that. I want to say that this tremendous superiority in numbers of nuclear warheads I have referred to in the early 1960s – 6000 or 7000 in the possession of NATO at a time when the Soviets had a few hundred (perhaps 400 to 500) – did not translate into usable military power. Therefore, if we wished to increase the military power of the West, as seemed desirable and necessary at the time, we would have to do it by recognising that we needed to increase *conventional* forces, and that we could not use, militarily, this tremendous nuclear force. I think it is becoming increasingly questionable whether the threat of initiating the use of nuclear weapons can deter one's opponent – in this case the Warsaw Pact – from initiating the use of conventional force. As I have said, I cannot conceive, nor can five of the seven retired British Chiefs of Defence Staff conceive, how NATO could initiate the use of nuclear weapons *in response to a Soviet conventional attack* with advantage to NATO. If that is the case, the threat of such response to Soviet conventional attack becomes less and less credible, and therefore less and less of a deterrent to that conventional attack.

CHARLTON: By the mid-1960s, the Kennedy Administration and later Lyndon Johnson had decided to freeze the numbers of American ICBMs. Why was that?

McNAMARA: Because we believed in what I am going to call deterrence, in 'assured destruction', and we felt we could achieve that strategic objective with the number of missiles and warheads we then had. We did not think of superiority of numbers turning unusable into usable military power. We believed then, as I believe today, that these warheads are not weapons; they have no military purpose; they cannot be used in war. They can only be used to deter the other side's initiation of a military strike, a nuclear strike; and if that's the objective, a limited number will accomplish it.

SO IT WAS WITH A mixture of anguish and resolution that Robert McNamara arrived at the doctrine of 'mutual assured destruction' (MAD) – the strange mental universe that we inhabit today, with its prospect of a man-made Day of Judgment, the intellectual impasse from which the Strategic Defence Initiative, or 'Star Wars', makes claim to deliver us. Until then we live in a state of mind which might be compared to that of the primitive Church, of which Edward Gibbon wrote, in *The History of the Decline and Fall of the Roman Empire*, that 'the influence of truth was very powerfully strengthened by an opinion that the world was coming to an end.' This opinion, the great historian went on to say, 'however it may deserve respect for its usefulness and antiquity has not, on the whole, proved agreeable to experience . . .'

    MAD, the theory of deterrence, in which all-out war is replaced by a protracted duel of moral attrition and the threat of retaliation, leaves the answer to a major issue wrapped in ambiguity. What is left of the deterring threat of nuclear weapons once we arrive at stability in the form of a guarantee of mutual assured destruction? This was the question President Kennedy raised, and he answered it by undertaking limited war in Vietnam. That failure of limited war as a deterrent has returned us, in more recent years, to technological innovations designed to reinforce the paramountcy of nuclear weapons in determining the outcome. How did Kennedy mean to avoid (as he put it) the free world being nibbled to death in a nuclear stalemate?

DEAN RUSK: The United States has not chosen to play the role of the world's policeman; we have not accepted any kind of global responsibility in that direction. Since World War II, there have been something over four hundred situations of violence somewhere in the world, and the US has been directly involved in seven or eight of those. We have to keep our eyes on those points of genuine vital interest to the United States, and make it clear that we are prepared to take action to defend those vital interests. But there will be a good many quarrels and changes in different parts of the world which are simply not our business.

However, I think these forty years without the use of nuclear weapons are no sure guarantee for the future. We and the Russians must try to avoid playing the game that Americans call the game of 'chicken' – to see how far one or the other can go without crossing that lethal line – because there can always be mistakes and misjudgments.

The most important thing that could be said about this post-war period is that, in this year of 1985, we shall have put behind us forty years since the firing of a nuclear weapon in anger, and despite the many – and often dangerous – crises we've had since 1945. President Kennedy helped to add to those years. I think we've learned, during that forty years, that the fingers on the nuclear triggers are *not* itchy, just waiting for a pretext to fire these dreadful weapons.

CHARLTON: What was the impact on Kennedy of Khruschev's often violent and provocative speeches? Here is Khruschev to the Supreme Soviet in June 1960: 'Every sober thinker is well aware that the danger from atomic and hydrogen bombs is greatest for countries with a high population density . . .' by which he clearly means the United States and Western Europe. 'We would suffer greatly, but *we* would survive'. And again, 'We are several years ahead of other countries in the design and mass production of intercontinental ballistic rockets. Our high rate of growth is no longer questioned. The only question is how much faster we're moving ahead than the United States.'

RUSK: I think President Kennedy looked upon that as rhetoric designed for a home audience. He was much more concerned about a speech Khruschev made, later than that, about 'wars of liberation', and also their definition of peaceful co-existence, which was – in their words – a continuation of a struggle by all means short of war. That is not the synonym for détente as we in the West understand the word. So he was concerned about that. But, on the other hand, President Kennedy and his senior advisers felt that it was just too late in history for the nuclear powers to pursue a policy of total hostility across the board. So, despite the serious Berlin crisis of 1961–2, and the extraordinarily dangerous Cuban missile crisis, we set in chain things which produced the Nuclear Test Ban Treaty of 1963; a consular agreement; a civil air agreement providing flights between New York and Moscow; two important space treaties; the launching of the Anti-Ballistic Missile Treaty; the Non-Proliferation Treaty, and other things. Whatever the Russians think of us – or we think of the Russians – somehow, at the end of the day, we and they will have to find a way to inhabit this speck of dust in the universe at the same time.

CHARLTON: But would you agree that, for the Soviet Union, nuclear parity had a political as well as a strategic value, that it offered the possibility of Soviet expansionism – the very thing which you tell us greatly concerned Kennedy, and which was explicit in the 'wars of liberation' speech that Khruschev made?

RUSK: There comes a point where one has to think of Henry Kissinger's remark – 'What in the name of heaven is nuclear superiority?' – because the scale of destructive power is so enormous that minor differences in numbers make no difference from the military point of view. The numbers have to be watched because they could affect perceptions in people's minds about what these numbers mean. If the Soviet Union ever felt that it had such large numbers that it could engage in adventures in many places without any kind of reaction from the rest of us, then we could have some dangers.

CHARLTON: Can you consider for a moment how it seemed to you *at the time* that the ratio of nuclear strength did affect the outcome of crisis? Take the Berlin crisis of 1961–2, and Kennedy's famous pronouncement there, '*Ich bin ein Berliner*'. Why did that crisis end peacefully?

RUSK: Sir Alec Douglas-Home and I decided that we had to follow up, with Gromyko, that Vienna Summit between Khruschev and Kennedy. And he and I decided that we would talk just as long and just as repetitively as did Mr Gromyko. We just talked and talked. Eventually I think we succeeded in talking some of the fever out of the problem. We had to say to them at that time, 'If you want war, you can have war in five minutes. All you've got to do is to start one. But if you don't want war, we'd better talk about this some more.' I think we reached a point where the Berlin issue did not loom as importantly in Khruschev's mind as it had in June 1961, and therefore that matter was wound up.

CHARLTON: But how important was the nuclear equation? Many took the view that because Berlin could be defended only by going to extremes, therefore it would be lost. Why did some Americans fear this would happen? Wasn't the *only* way to respond to the Berlin crisis a nuclear response?

RUSK: There was a graduated response in the contingency plans of NATO with respect to Berlin. My own hunch is that somewhere along the way the matter would have been resolved before we got to the nuclear stage, because neither side could possibly want war – and that includes the Russians.

CHARLTON: But doesn't that argue that the nuclear factor *is* the ultimate determinant in the manipulation of risk and crisis?

RUSK: It does suppose some limits beyond which one does *not* go, one *must* not go. We have learned that in forty years, and I hope very much that our successors will keep that in mind, in both Moscow and Washington.

CHARLTON: What about Cuba? If one recalls Clausewitz's simple formula, 'the effect that a certain step will have on the enemy' is the most relevant of all the factors in the action. What is it possible to add, after all these years, to our knowledge of why Khruschev and the Politburo challenged President Kennedy with nuclear weapons on America's doorstep in Cuba?

RUSK: I don't believe that we ever knew with precision just why Mr Khruschev decided to put the missiles in Cuba, or why he thought that he could do so without a very strong American reaction. It may be that he made the judgment that, since President Kennedy had not followed up the Bay of Pigs with American forces, we would not attach much importance to Cuba. It may be that the advantages to him of getting a hundred of these missiles in Cuba would be so great that it would be worth taking a chance if there were only a twenty per cent chance of success. Whatever the reasons, we felt that the missiles in Cuba from a military point of view would make it possible for them to knock out our Strategic Air Command bases with almost no advance warning. From a political point of view, the effects in the Western hemisphere and in NATO would be devastating. So that produced an extraordinarily dangerous crisis.

CHARLTON: What is the determinant? Is it the central nuclear balance? Why did he do that when America was in the position (perhaps stronger then than it is today) to answer from terms of superiority?

RUSK: I can't document this point, but I feel rather strongly that somehow Cuba was connected with Berlin in Khruschev's mind, that Khruschev had in mind that he would get these missiles into Cuba very quickly and secretly and then, much more forcefully, at that point call attention to these missiles in Cuba as a makeweight argument over Berlin. I can't go into all the details of why I've come to that conclusion, but I think the Cuban missiles were related to his pressures on Berlin.

THE EVENTS OF 1962 ARE still the most dramatic of our nuclear era. Why Nikita Khruschev ignored Kennedy's formal warnings with his dynamic thrust to position nuclear armed missiles on America's doorstep, why he then gave way, and what impact the central nuclear balance had upon the seminal crises of Cuba and Berlin – there is no unanimous American view. What has today become the ascendant branch of American strategic thinking would contest Robert McNamara's relegation of the role played by nuclear weapons in shaping the outcome of crisis and the exercise of risk.

ROBERT McNAMARA: I didn't believe then, and I don't believe today, that it did affect the outcome of crises. Once one had a sufficient force to deter one's opponents from initiating the use of nuclear weapons, 'your' nuclear force or 'our' nuclear force had no impact on actions in a political crisis.

CHARLTON: Why did the Berlin crisis of 1962 have a peaceful outcome when it was beyond the reach of conventional forces to intervene?

McNAMARA: That's a very good question. It was not because we had the superiority I referred to – say, 6000 strategic warheads in NATO to (perhaps) 200 to 400 Warsaw Pact warheads. The very fact that, in the face of that NATO strategic superiority, the Soviets moved against Berlin is, I think, an illustration of my point.

CHARLTON: What about Cuba, the classic crisis?

McNAMARA: I would make the same point in the case of Cuba. The Soviets, again in the face of tremendous US strategic nuclear superiority at the time of Cuba – probably in the order of 7000 warheads to maybe 400 or 500 Soviet warheads – took a very aggressive move introducing missiles in Cuba. They were finally forced out, but it was not through the threat of use of nuclear weapons. We never conceived of using nuclear weapons under those circumstances. It was our tremendous conventional power in the region which forced the Soviets to take those missiles out.

CHARLTON: But until the Kremlin archives are opened, that must remain, if I may suggest it, a unilateral assumption on your part, mustn't it?

McNAMARA: Well, I've had some conversations with Soviets in the intervening years, and they confirm that view.

CHARLTON: How should one interpret what we know Mr Kuznetsov (the Soviet Deputy Foreign Minister) said to John J. McCloy in the United States very shortly after the Cuban crisis: 'You will never be able to do this to us again!' Surely that would suggest that Khruschev backed down, having taken a hazardous risk, in the face of America's strategic superiority?

McNAMARA: No, I think one can interpret Kuznetsov's words in different ways. But I think what he meant – and Soviet actions since that time would lend support to my interpretation – is that they would never again place themselves in a weak position militarily vis-à-vis the US or NATO.

CHARLTON: But the reality is the implied, perhaps secret threat of using nuclear weapons if there's an attempt to tilt the balance. Why did Khruschev, when that balance was so clearly in favour of the United States, take the risk he did?

McNAMARA: I don't know. That's a very good question. I have no answer to it. And I have not found a Russian, by the way, who has an answer.

PRESIDENT KENNEDY HELD OUT against Khruschev's violent pressure. That the Soviets, certainly retrospectively, had looked hard at the nuclear equation would seem to be confirmed in Dean Rusk's response to the question, 'Why did Khruschev give way in Cuba?'

DEAN RUSK: I think he recognised that the United States had overwhelming conventional superiority in the vicinity of Cuba (our state of Florida was about to sink under the sea with the weight of military power we assembled there), and that his only response would almost *have* to be in the nuclear field. We did not believe that Chairman Khruschev would launch a nuclear strike because of Cuba, but we could not *know* it for certain. So we had to take that into account. But, fortunately, Mr Khruschev kept his wits about him and did not allow that matter to escalate into general war.

CHARLTON: Did you subsequently come to the view that the Soviet Union attributed their failure in Cuba not just to the reality of America's conventional superiority – Florida, as you've said, about to sink under it – but, in the end, to their own *nuclear* inferiority?

RUSK: We had some reason to believe, afterwards, that the Soviets thought we had counted missiles at the time of the Cuban missile crisis. In fact, we had not. Apparently they thought so, because shortly after that crisis a high Russian official[1] said to Mr John J. McCloy in New York, 'Well, Mr McCloy, you got away with it this time. You'll never get away with it again!' If you take into account the lead time required for making decisions and doing all the preparatory work and so forth, much of their further deployment of nuclear weapons in later years undoubtedly came from decisions made shortly after the Cuban missile crisis.

CUBA WAS A CRUCIAL MOMENT in world history. Compounding the effect of Stalin's actions in Eastern Europe at the end of World War II, it profoundly shocked the Americans. Kennedy had appeared much stronger in Berlin – where the nuclear guarantee was less equivocal – than he had in Cuba, hitherto only a flank to the central design of American strategy, which lay in Europe. The reason was perhaps (as Dean Rusk suggested) that, because Kennedy had not been prepared to push the abortive Bay of Pigs invasion to its logical conclusion, the resolute gambler in the Kremlin had seen Cuba as Kennedy's (and America's) Achilles heel. Fidel Castro acknowledged that the Soviet rockets in Cuba were meant, as he put it, 'to strengthen the Socialist camp as a whole'. In other words, they were to provide the Soviet Union with an inexpensive means of altering the balance of power in its favour.

Khruschev's adventure was a challenge to the whole edifice of deterrence and its premise that rivalry between nuclear powers can, and must, be pursued without head-on confrontation. Reflection on how close the world had come to 'the lightning flash in a clear sky' concentrated all minds, and also changed them. By most accounts it changed Robert McNamara's. In the 1960s, around Moscow, the Russians had been the first (they remain the only ones) to deploy defences against nuclear

[1] agreed by Robert McNamara (see page 23) to be the Deputy Foreign Minister, Kuznetsov

attack. Doctrinally, such a concept conflicted with McNamara's evangelism for deterrence on the certainty of 'mutual assured destruction'. At that time the Americans were developing – but had not *deployed* – a defence against ballistic missiles. Deterrence required, as a fundamental condition, the ability to penetrate any defence in order to assure the threat of retaliation. In consequence, what many believe to be the single most destabilising development in the history of the nuclear arms competition – the placing of many warheads on a single rocket in order to saturate and overwhelm defences, the hydra-headed missile MIRV – was being conceived.

ROBERT MCNAMARA: The MIRV development, MIRV research, began roughly in 1966. Of course, as you know, the MIRVs weren't deployed until sometime around 1972. It's a very interesting development because it is an illustration of this action-reaction phenomenon that I think is so important to recognise as stimulating moves by the Soviets and ourselves. MIRV research was started as an answer by the US to the Soviet anti-ballistic missile deployment which they were beginning, which we had evidence of, and which they did not deny. We knew that they were proceeding to deploy it around Moscow. What we did not know was the degree to which they intended to deploy it across the rest of the Soviet Union. It's an illustration of this problem of uncertainty.

We had to assume, since we saw them starting, that they would continue. If they did, we of necessity would have to maintain our deterrent – our insurance that we had the capability under all circumstances to absorb a Soviet nuclear strike and survive with sufficient nuclear weapons to inflict unacceptable damage on them. That was our basis for concluding that we could deter them from ever initiating that strike. If they're building defence, then we would of necessity have to increase our *offensive* forces. To do that, we concluded, the best, the most efficient, the most functional way was to add so-called 'multiple independently targeted re-entry vehicles' to our launchers – that's what MIRV means. And therefore we began the research to develop those.

We recognised at the time we started MIRV research in the mid-1960s that, if it ever came to deployment, it was a dangerous technology to deploy because the Soviets could ultimately follow it in five or ten years. Then we would have both sides at a much higher numerical level and perhaps a much less stable level. So it was assumed at the time we started research that we would never *deploy* it, *if* the Soviets agreed to stop deployment of their ABM. They *ultimately* did so – several years later, in 1972. But for a variety of reasons the US went ahead and deployed its MIRVs. Since that time the Soviets have followed, and we do have each side today at much higher and much less stable levels.

CHARLTON: But as a matter of historical record, many people seem to have felt that it was you who gave a powerful impetus to MIRV development earlier in the 1960s with your declaration of a 'counterforce' strategy to attack Soviet military targets. This increased the number of targets and therefore the plausibility of multiple warheads to cope with the extra targets.

McNAMARA: No. It's perhaps natural that people might come to that conclusion, but I think it is wrong in fact, as I recall. There was absolutely no connection between counterforce strategy on one hand and MIRVs. The MIRV research was initiated *solely* as a means of countering Soviet anti-ballistic missile deployment.

THE SOVIET ANTI-BALLISTIC MISSILE deployment in the 1960s created, as Robert McNamara saw it, new and irrational uncertainties. Their contribution to that fear of the Apocalypse to which all in the White House at the time of Cuba attest – together with the deepening involvement in Vietnam, where the Americans had determined to reinforce deterrence by answering limited war with limited war – was hastening McNamara down his chosen path. He decided the time had come to try to reconcile this dialectic of opposing nuclear weapons and political wills – and was instrumental in persuading President Lyndon B. Johnson to take an initiative with the Russians – in the hope that they would come to share the American insight into the nature of nuclear deterrence. The opportunity was taken at the summit meeting at Glassboro, New Jersey, in 1967 between President Johnson and the Soviet Premier, Alexei Kosygin. McNamara made a passionate plea to Kosygin concerning the nature of the Soviet Union's nuclear capabilities – and intentions.

ROBERT McNAMARA: We had great difficulty in determining what they subscribed to. At that point, most of the Soviet military writing that we had access to indicated that they believed that *any* military conflict between East and West would be a *nuclear* conflict. Quite frankly, their writings made no sense to us, and that was particularly true as the size of their force increased. By 1967, when they were proceeding to deploy their anti-ballistic missile defence, we found it impossible to rationalise their writings and their actions. In 1967, President Johnson met Prime Minister Kosygin in Glassboro and confronted him with the way we interpreted their actions, particularly as they related to anti-ballistic missile defence. Kosygin could no more understand our reactions than we could understand his. The two sides had totally different views of the nuclear world they lived in at that time.

CHARLTON: Would you accept this, from a source with whom you may not willingly wish to agree? President Nixon says this:

> In American thinking, strategic nuclear superiority and the attempt to limit damage in the event of nuclear war were replaced by theories of deterrence that emphasise the inevitability of mass civilian destruction, assured destruction. These theories were linked with an arms-control-oriented belief that nuclear weapons beyond the necessary minimum lacked political or military utility. Whereas the Soviet Union did not separate

deterrence and defence, but oriented their planning towards their ability to fight and survive and win a nuclear war . . .

MCNAMARA: I think that states very clearly both my view of our strategy of 1967 and my view of the Soviet strategy at that time.

CHARLTON: In other words, the Soviet Union's analysis (and the reason Kosygin does not agree with Johnson at Glassboro) is that the Soviets *do* perceive a political utility in the nuclear weapons which your rational minds do not acknowledge.

MCNAMARA: No, I don't want to put those words in Kosygin's mouth at that time. What I want to say is that I don't believe Kosygin understood the way we looked at deterrence. At one point Johnson turned to me and said, 'Bob, you explain to Kosygin how we view their anti-ballistic missile deployment.'

I said, 'Mr Prime Minister, you must understand that we will maintain a deterrent under any circumstances. And we view a deterrent as a nuclear force so strong that it can absorb your nuclear attack on it and survive with sufficient power to inflict unacceptable damage on you. And, therefore, if you put a defence in place, we're going to have to expand our nuclear *offensive* forces. You may think, as the Congress apparently does, that a proper response to the Soviet defence is a US defence; but I tell you the proper response – and it will *be* our response – is to expand our offensive force . . .'

He absolutely erupted. He became red in the face. He pounded the table. He said, 'Defence is moral, offence is immoral.' I think that is what he believed. This was not a show; he believed it. Perhaps his military commanders also believed that you could use nuclear weapons in war and exchange nuclear shots, and ultimately the side with the largest number would prevail and 'win' the war – whatever that meant.

I don't know that Kosygin believed that. But he clearly had an erroneous view, in our minds, and, I think, quite a different view then than his counterparts today have of what is reality in the nuclear age and what each side needs to maintain security. That is deterrence. He did not understand it; his view was quite different from ours; his counterparts today would agree one hundred per cent with the way *we* expressed it in 1967.

ALMOST TWENTY YEARS AGO, Robert McNamara urged upon the Russians that nations should not aspire to defend their peoples against the Bomb, but rather to make the weapon *itself* invulnerable – that to attempt defence would inevitably mean only more and more offensive weapons. This is one root criticism of President Reagan's SDI ('Star Wars') proposal today. As we shall see subsequently, the proponents of the SDI believe they will be able to justify a different verdict in the years ahead.

But that American initiative, at Glassboro in 1967, to forsake the anti-ballistic missile was the first practical step in seeking Soviet co-operation for the proposition that human survival in the nuclear age would depend largely on two things – the rational intelligence of state leadership, and arms control. There was at first no response. A year later, in 1968, the Soviet Union invaded Czechoslovakia and put an end to the 'Prague Spring', the attempt to reform the Soviet-imposed model of Communist orthodoxy. A new shadow was thrown on the cave wall.

Not until the newly elected American government took office could this diplomacy concerning nuclear weapons be revived and later carried into effect. The Anti-Ballistic Missile Treaty became part of the system of rewards and punishments conceived by Dr Henry Kissinger in his attempt to 'manage' the emergence of the Soviet Union as a superpower and to secure 'deterrence through détente'.

★ 2 ★
DETERRENCE THROUGH DÉTENTE:

The Hand of Henry Kissinger

WHEN PRESIDENT NIXON took office in 1969, he spoke at once of the unique and fatal implications which nuclear weapons possess for the statesman. 'While I would like', he said, 'to provide the American people with complete protection against nuclear attack, it is not now within our power to do so . . .' The President added, 'It might look to an opponent like the prelude to an offensive strategy threatening the Soviet deterrent.'

President Nixon was reiterating the essence of Robert McNamara's passionate presentation to the Soviet Premier, Mr Kosygin, at the Glassboro summit two years earlier. To attempt a nuclear defence would merely mean an intensified race in *offensive* weapons to overpower that defence, and, therefore, 'Mutual assured destruction' – assuring the certain threat of retaliation in kind – should be acknowledged as the rational prescription for stable deterrence. It fell to the Nixon Administration to bring about the fascinating and fitful negotiation with the Soviet Union which was to give a cold and ambiguous assent to Robert McNamara's proposition.

The Strategic Arms Limitation Talks (SALT) became the principal arena for a struggle which was itself a substitute for war. SALT was compared, in the beginning, to the Congress of Vienna in the last century, which secured the forty years of peace that followed the Napoleonic Wars. The similarities were superficially beguiling. What Talleyrand had said of his colleagues and former allies against Napoleon, that they were 'too frightened to fight one another, too stupid to agree', was given a wholly new dimension by the nuclear competition. The Russians were achieving nuclear parity with the United States. The balance of power was being challenged.

In 1968, the year Nixon was elected, the Russians had reasserted their hegemony in Europe by invading Czechoslovakia. In South Vietnam, the Communist forces (armed by the Soviet Union) had launched the 'Tet' offensive in more than forty provincial towns. Their ability to do so was seen in America at the time as overthrowing certain basic assumptions about the nature and progress of the war in Vietnam. In consequence, amid a growing domestic tumult, President Johnson decided not to seek re-election. As President Nixon drove down Pennsylvania Avenue from Capitol Hill on his inauguration day, the last image that he can have taken with him into office, as his car turned the corner by the White House, was of some stands of hostile demonstrators against the Vietnam War, waving the Viet Cong flag and chanting the name of Ho Chi Minh, the Communist leader with whose insurgent armies the United States was at war. There was grave public disquiet – and at the gates of the White House itself.

Into this forbidding context stepped Dr Henry Kissinger, with his immense talents and intelligence. For almost ten years he was to be one of the most powerful men in the world. In his own book about the Congress of Vienna, Dr Kissinger had written of those statesmen who achieved final greatness that it was given to them 'not only to maintain the perfection of order but to have the strength to contemplate chaos – and there to find the material for fresh creation'. How far did chaos appear to Henry Kissinger himself to be the prospect, as he went to the White House as President Nixon's National Security Adviser and later his Secretary of State?

HENRY KISSINGER: It was a very difficult period, because the bipartisan consensus that had characterised US foreign policy for most of the post-war period was collapsing. A kind of opposition was developing in the United States that was unprecedented. The practical proposals that were being made had the consequence of a complete collapse of a military effort in Vietnam that our predecessors had started and which had left us with 550,000 troops in place. (Our studies indicated, for example, that it would take us eighteen months to get them out, even as a simple logistics problem.) This was combined with an attack on every military programme, together with the fact that the people who had created the conditions went into opposition to what were their own policies as soon as they were out of office. So it was an extremely complicated situation, not eased by the fact that President Nixon (who was a man of great accomplishment and great knowledge in foreign policy) did not have the art of gaining popular support the way, for example, President Reagan has.

CHARLTON: The 'strength to contemplate chaos', you said, 'there to find the material for fresh creation . . .' Why was arms control, SALT, the material for fresh creation as you saw it, and to become the principal activity for what you called 'a new structure of peace' with the Soviet Union?

KISSINGER: That was not our policy. Our policy was much more complicated than this. Arms control to us (that is, to Nixon and me, and to those who dominated the Nixon Administration) was not an end in itself.

It was one of the tools, and in fact we did not make even the first preliminary agreement on arms control until May 1971, which was two-plus years after we came into office. Our strategy was to try to bring China into play; to try to isolate North Vietnam; to establish a new relationship with Europe and with the Soviet Union; to move ahead on a broad front. We believed in 'linkage'. We, for example, did not agree to any increase in trade until there had been some preliminary agreement on arms control. So we never believed that arms control by itself could carry the whole burden of East-West relations. There were, however, significant segments of American public opinion (especially scientific and intellectual opinion) who thought exactly that; and since they were needed to carry any agreement through the Congress against conservative opposition, they tended to have a more vocal role than our theory would have justified.

HENRY KISSINGER HAD AN overarching concept of grand strategy. His enticing of China out of its years of self-imposed isolation and the dialogue he established with the leaders of the Soviet Union have written some of the most important history of the twentieth century. Kissinger declared that the problem of the age was how to 'manage' the emergence of the Soviet Union as a superpower. That relationship turned fundamentally on the supreme instruments of national power and sovereignty – nuclear weapons.

As the Strategic Arms Limitation Talks began, the Soviet military programme was gaining momentum. (Dean Rusk has already drawn our attention, in the first chapter, to the decisions the Russians had taken in the aftermath of the Cuban missile crisis.) For their part, the Americans had stopped building ICBMs, for the reasons Robert McNamara has given, and were now trying 'not to lose' rather than to win in Vietnam. There was evident concern about the long-term trends in the Soviet strategic advance. Kissinger believed that, as nuclear parity approached, it was the duty of the statesman to dominate what he could not avoid. That was also the intention of President Nixon, as the chief American negotiator with the Russians at these first SALT talks, Gerard Smith, recalls.

GERARD SMITH: Neither side is going to let the other get a superior position. I think Nixon was sensible enough to realise that the best we could do would be to register parity, and not let the Soviets get into an overreaching position.
CHARLTON: But on the specific point of superiority, written into the Republican Party platform today as it was in the 1950s with President Eisenhower and Secretary John Foster Dulles – did Nixon yield on that for essentially the same reason Eisenhower himself did, that it could no longer be made a continuing requirement of American policy?
SMITH: I suspect that Eisenhower had a much clearer notion of what was possible than Nixon. You speak of Eisenhower talking about superiority.

My clearest recollection is that, early on, he accepted a doctrine of 'sufficiency'. It was at the instance of a man named Don Quarles, who was Deputy Secretary of Defence. They articulated this very clearly. They said that after a certain number of weapons – no matter what the other side has – you don't need more. It is quite clear that sufficiency was guiding the President's decisions in the late 1950s.

CHARLTON: Was that also true of President Nixon?

SMITH: I felt he had not thought this through as carefully as Eisenhower had. I think he felt that the Soviets were moving faster in the strategic field than we were, and that maybe this was the last time (in 1969, 1970, 1971) that we could deal with the Soviets on an equivalent basis. So it did not come to his mind as sufficiency so much as to stop the Soviets from going ahead pell-mell.

CHARLTON: What, at first hand, did you note of Nixon's view as to whether it was politically or economically possible for the United States, at that time, to build and deploy more major strategic weapons systems?

SMITH: We were seeing then what we are seeing now. There was a strong revulsion in large segments of the populus to a continuing upward spiral. I think Nixon as a politician realised that his chances of getting large appropriations for weapons systems depended, substantially, on offering to *control* arms. That is what I think we're seeing now. The Reagan Administration knows that if it was not in a position of offering to *reduce* strategic arms, it could not get the Congress to approve *increases* in strategic arms. It's quite a paradox.

CHARLTON: To what extent, as President Nixon negotiated the first SALT agreement with his Soviet opposite numbers, was he (in the French diplomatic formulation) '*demandeur*'?

SMITH: We never had the sense of being '*demandeur*' in the actual front lines. I felt that we had substantial qualitative advantages, even though the Soviet numbers were increasing and ours were not. We were on the verge of MIRV, the multiple independently targetable re-entry vehicles; the Soviets were not and would not be for some years. So the qualitative advantage, we thought (and I think correctly) lay with us.

CHARLTON: But '*demandeur*' perhaps in another sense, as the Soviet Union may have seen it, in that SALT I and the American decision to go ahead with that were recognition that there was no way, *other* than by an agreement to limit arms, that the Soviet Union could be prevented from achieving numerical superiority in offensive ballistic missiles?

SMITH: I think that is probably correct for that time. Now, given enough years ahead – it's no trick – we could always, if it was in our interest, build more of the current class of ballistic missile. But I think you're right in saying that in 1969–70, in the absence of arms control, the Soviets were going to have a larger number of launchers for their strategic forces than we were.

CHARLTON: If he conceded parity in the central nuclear balance to the

Soviet Union – as he did, symbolically, in the SALT agreement of 1972 –
what did President Nixon then feel would deter the Soviet Union from
political expansion elsewhere in the world? If the Soviet Union had
achieved an equality of power with the United States, was not the corollary
of that going to be expanding political opportunities?

SMITH: It was Kissinger's thesis that alongside the arms control
agreements there would be a network of agreements that it would be in the
interest of the Soviet Union to keep. I think Kissinger figured that if the
Soviets went around committing aggressions, they could not have these
other 'goodies' – and that would deter them.

KISSINGER'S GRAND DESIGN of judicious rewards and punishments as a
deterrent, embracing trade and technology and credits as well as arms
control, was critical to the nature of his discourse. Arms control by itself
could not relieve tensions. If it were not linked to restraint in worldwide
competition, Kissinger said, 'strategic arms control might become a safety
valve for Soviet expansionist designs – a vehicle for Soviet peace offen-
sives to mask or compensate for some new act of aggression. Every time
there was a Soviet aggressive move, there would be appeals that the new
tensions now made arms control talks even more important. This is why
I favoured linkage.'

But he was also convinced that the nuclear weapon had added a new
dimension of horror and, therefore, responsibility for national leaders.
To what extent did Kissinger consider that possession by both sides of
the 'absolute weapon' meant there could no longer be an 'absolute enemy' – an enemy whose ideology, or whose very existence, was a threat
to one's own existence or survival?

HENRY KISSINGER: I have always believed that Communism is morally
repugnant, and I think if you go through my writings you will never find
any deviation from that point of view. I have also believed that nuclear
weapons impose the necessity of co-existence. I do not base that co-
existence on any moral acceptance of the Soviet system, but on the
practical necessities that nuclear weapons create. That has been my
position from the very beginning. I wrote a book in 1956 called *Nuclear
Weapons and Foreign Policy* which was perhaps premature, but in which I
said that, sooner or later (I thought it would come sooner than it did),
strategic nuclear weapons would tend towards a kind of parity which
would make absolute war impossible; and I called for alternatives. I've
never changed that position. I believe that is still true now. Sometimes I
have changed my view as to what the alternatives could be, depending on
the technology of the moment, and I don't claim infallibility with respect
to technological alternatives – but that's not my function.

CHARLTON: How far did you take the view that nuclear threats were more
or less infallible in abolishing aggressive intentions?

KISSINGER: I've never believed that – I've believed exactly the opposite. I've believed that as nuclear parity was achieved, threats *other* than nuclear war would gain greater force, and that it was the obligation of the West to create obstacles to these other threats.

CHARLTON: Stability at the level of the nuclear balance created instability at other levels?

KISSINGER: Exactly.

CHARLTON: How, in your view, did the ratio of nuclear strength influence or dictate the outcome of crisis?

KISSINGER: I have always believed, contrary to many scientists, that you're better off with superiority than with parity. I have also thought that absolute superiority was going to become next to impossible to attain; either because it was no longer achievable technically, or because the calculations would be too complex for anybody to have any confidence in them. Nevertheless, this is one extreme. At the other extreme, however, I believed (and I still believe) that a strategy based on mass extermination of populations would lead to the gradual demoralisation of the West, and to the growth of the unilateral disarmament movement and pacifism. I do not think one can (or should) convince democratic publics that their extermination is the key element in their security, either the threat of *their* extermination or of *mutual* extermination. So my view was that we would be better off with superiority than with parity. Even if superiority was not attainable, we were better off with a capacity for discriminating targeting than with a capacity for indiscriminate destruction.

CHARLTON: You are reported as having said that parity with the Russians stopped you, in your time – over the Soviet attempt, in 1970, to establish a submarine base at Cienfuegos in Cuba – from adopting the same tactics as President Kennedy had during the Cuban crisis in 1962.

KISSINGER: I never said that. Absolutely not. We used more or less the same tactics and we achieved more or less the same result: that is, we achieved the dismantlement of what we thought was a Soviet nuclear submarine base, and which I believe *was* a Soviet nuclear submarine base.

CHARLTON: With the implicit nuclear threat in order to achieve that?

KISSINGER: We didn't need implicit nuclear threats any more than Kennedy did, because Cuba is so close to our shores. We blockaded the harbour of Cienfuegos. He blockaded the whole island – so he more or less used the same tactic.

CHARLTON: Does, therefore, the behaviour of states in the last analysis conform to the traditional pattern – once nuclear parity has been established?

KISSINGER: No – but I think whoever has a local advantage has a decided and very important advantage, precisely because the side that can extricate itself *only* by initiating the use of nuclear weapons is at a very great disadvantage.

AT THE HEART OF Henry Kissinger's discourse was his stated belief that, as the Soviet Union achieved nuclear parity, '. . . threats *other* than nuclear war would gain greater force', and that 'it was the obligation of the West to create obstacles to those other threats.' Kissinger laid subsequent failures of the détente policy to create those obstacles, as a deterrent to the extension of Communist power and Soviet influence in his own time, squarely at the door of 'the Watergate scandal'. The crippling of Presidential authority meant the loss of the capacity both to offer incentives for responsible behaviour and to apply inhibiting penalties for aggressive actions.

But there was also, perhaps, an underlying, unspoken reason. In Henry Kissinger's search for a stable world order were echoes of what Lord Castlereagh, the British Foreign Secretary and the soul of the coalition against Napoleon, had told the House of Commons about the Congress of Vienna: 'The Congress was not assembled for the discussion of moral principles, but for great practical purposes – to establish effectual provisions for the general security.' Kissinger was trying to wean American foreign policy away from both its traditional oscillations and its historical preoccupation with moral principles. Henry Kissinger's manipulations of the balance of power might have been familiar in the statesman's world of the Congress of Vienna, a context he was trying to recreate; but they were alien to much of the American body politic, to whom foreign policy is obliged to be, above all, a *public* policy subject to public scrutiny.

HENRY KISSINGER: Our style of foreign policy would have been easily understood in Britain, but was not easy to understand in the United States. We believed in a national-interest-based foreign policy. You did not have to explain in Great Britain through the eighteenth and nineteenth centuries the problem of throwing Britain's weight to whoever seemed the weaker of the continental countries, and Britain made no *moral* claim for that. For the United States this was a rather novel approach.

At the precise moment that we had achieved apparent success, both at isolating Vietnam and in relations with China and the Soviet Union, there occurred 'Watergate', a totally unpredictable event which collapsed executive authority, so that for fifteen to eighteen months the locus of executive respect by the public was the State Department – which was unheard of. That then put us into a much more defensive posture, so by 1975, we had a coalition of conservatives and liberals against the policy that Nixon and later Ford were carrying out, with me as Secretary of State. You had liberals who felt that if Nixon was for peace, confrontation could not be all bad, and conservatives who believed that any deal with the Soviets was wicked.

CHARLTON: On the point of the moralistic aspects of the American political tradition, you've written of the time when you came to office that, for the United States, conflict is unnatural. It was seen as caused by evil men or motives. Thus the Soviet Union as a tyranny fulfilled the traditional image of irreconcilable conflict as between good and evil.

KISSINGER: You have two extremes in America. Since conflict is considered unnatural, one of two things happens: either the opponent is considered inherently evil, or it is believed that the opponent has undergone a conversion and is, therefore, ready for a final settlement – without being able to express what the content of the final settlement is.

CHARLTON: But if Americans saw relations between states as either peaceful or warlike, in black and white terms, why did you think, if that *was* the American political tradition, that it had become incompatible with the American national interest and a sound foreign policy?

KISSINGER: Because, at the end of the day, the relationship among states has to be able to be expressed in some concrete conditions. If you cannot express it in concrete conditions, you are doomed to oscillate between extremes of conciliation and extremes of intransigence, overdo each of them as you go through each phase, and then be disappointed with each phase. The attempt that President Nixon and I made, inconclusively, was to see whether we could express conditions of peace or stability in some specific manner, and this more or less runs counter to the American tradition. Go back to American post-war history; take the policy of containment. You will find Dean Acheson, Dulles, Truman and Eisenhower always saying that when we have positions of strength, the negotiating position will improve. What we were going to *do* with the negotiating position – what we were going to *ask* of the Russians if they came to the conference table – I defy anybody to find one statement.

DR KISSINGER'S CREATIVE AND COHERENT substitute for this long-standing omission was his policy of entangling the Soviet Union in a web of involvements on arms agreements, trade and credits, to be linked to restraint by the Russians in the exercise of Lenin's ambition for the Soviet state as a power fulfilling a millennial mission. However, among Kissinger's more compelling domestic critics were those who felt there should be more to these involvements than the principle of agreement on a set of rules, and that what was missing from his concept was an ethic of a peaceful order. Otherwise why resist the revolutionary power?

Liberals who felt that détente condoned the suppression of human rights and conservatives who baulked at notions of equality or parity with the Soviet Union combined under the leadership of a powerful Senator, Henry ('Scoop') Jackson. This formidable opposition in the Congress consistently attacked both the arithmetic and the concept of the SALT talks and all but wrecked the policy. One of the Americans who sat with Kissinger across the table from the Russian leaders during the SALT negotiations, as a member of the National Security Council, was Hal Sonnenfeldt.

HELMUT SONNENFELDT: The parity notions that existed, in the Administration at least, fifteen years ago in the early 1970s, did not mean that the Soviets would be left risk-free to pursue their various objectives and purposes. That particular presumption, that underlying premise of détente (and indeed of the whole détente regime) was not borne out in the event, partly because the Americans were so divided that we had problems defining what our interests and commitments were. We had difficulty getting our defence budgets through Congress and the Soviets made it very clear that, as far as *they* were concerned, the Third World was an arena for continued geo-political manoeuvre. That's really what brought about the disenchantment with détente and the widespread criticism in the United States in the later part of the 1970s and into this decade.

CHARLTON: SALT I was approved by the Senate only after Senator Jackson's amendment to the treaty was passed, asking the President to seek a future treaty that would not limit the United States to levels of these missiles which were inferior to limits for the Soviet Union. What underlay that objection was a differing perception of power – and the political exercise of power through these weapons – which clearly was not resolved in the USA?

SONNENFELDT: We had no consensus in this country, and there were a lot of people (including Senator Jackson, and many in the Republican Party as well) who believed that the Anti-Ballistic Missile Agreement might have been unwise. They saw more promise in the possibilities of defence and saw us, the Americans, giving up in an area where technologically we might well have had an advantage over the Soviets.

Secondly, people were unhappy about the seeming disparities that were incorporated in the SALT I *offence* agreement, which gave the Soviets substantially larger numbers of submarines for sea-launched ballistic missiles. It also gave them, or legitimised, their very substantial advantage in land-based ICBMs, and that produced the Jackson Amendment to which you refer, calling for *equality* in future agreements – without, however, defining precisely how that equality would be constituted. But I think the dominant argument really had to do with the political appearance.

There was one issue, however, a military issue (at least to a very considerable degree) which has really bedevilled the whole process of negotiating strategic arms limitations with the Soviets. Because of their large land-based forces, the Soviet capacity to threaten the totality of *our* land-based force of Minutemen was seen on the horizon in 1972 and became essentially a fact by, let us say, 1980. Whereas a comparable American capability to threaten a large portion, or the entirety, of the Soviet land-based missile force has still not been achieved to this day. Now, whether that presents real military options or not is a matter of constant argument. But that was a very powerful military component in what was, basically, an agreement about the *political* and *psychological* dangers of the appearance of inequality, and the expected Soviet ability to translate that advantage into political gains. The argument is endless whether the Soviets in Angola, and in Ethiopia, and later in Afghanistan were exploiting the appearance of strategic advantage.

CHARLTON: Whereas Henry Kissinger, and you, for example, took the view that those numerical advantages were illusory . . .

SONNENFELDT: We took the view that we could live with numerical disadvantages, especially as regards launchers, for a period of time. But, of course, one of the great disappointments of SALT I was that the clear assumption that there would *then* be substantial cutbacks in offensive forces (on which, incidentally, the Anti-Ballistic Missile Agreement was also based) was an assumption never borne out by subsequent events.

THE EMERGENCE OF THIS particular Soviet advantage in heavy land-based missiles, and the question of whether it stimulated the possibility of political transfers, had returned the American debate to an earlier apprehension, recalling President Kennedy's words in 1960. Reflecting upon the likely consequences of the sudden advent of Sputnik, the world's first intercontinental ballistic missile, he said:

> Soviet missile power will be the shield from behind which they will slowly but surely advance through 'Sputnik' diplomacy, limited wars and the vicious blackmail of our allies. The periphery of the free world will be nibbled away . . .

The argument gathered force following President Nixon's decline and fall and became a major factor in the change of climate over the following years which led to the election of President Reagan. How Moscow saw the American condition at the time of the SALT negotiations and the Anti-Ballistic Missile Treaty in 1972, which were coincidental with the last stages of the American engagement in Vietnam, has naturally aroused a good deal of scholarly interest and historical speculation. As Henry Kissinger looked back to those perceptions, do they not show that the Russians had come to see an underlying change in the balance of power and a comparative (if transient) American weakness?

HENRY KISSINGER: Absolutely not! Considering that we had riots in the streets, that we were involved in a war in Vietnam, that the opposition party held both houses of the Congress, I think we achieved an extraordinary flexibility of foreign policy. After all, we reduced Soviet influence in the Middle East even *after* Watergate. I don't think the Soviet Union looked on the Nixon Administration as a weak opponent. I think they looked at us as a formidable opponent – we 'opened' to China in the middle of all our travails (which must have been an extremely un-settling time for the Soviet Union) – and what opportunity did they seize during that period? As long as Nixon was even relatively unimpaired we made progress in negotiations with the Soviets, lost no international position, and in fact made great gains in the Middle East.

CHARLTON: But wouldn't you agree it is a period seen today as the prelude to a series of global adventures by the Soviet Union?

KISSINGER: It was a prelude to a series of global adventures for a whole variety of reasons. First, because with the collapse of our executive authority, starting in 1973, we destroyed a President. We then had a McGovernite Congress. The people who were defeated in 1972, by the most overwhelming majority but one in American history, regained Congress as a result of events that had absolutely nothing to do with the political process. As a result of this, there was the oddest coalition between liberals and conservatives who took away both the carrot and the stick. They prevented us from resisting Soviet aggression in Angola. At the same time they challenged the Soviet Union with the Jackson and the Stevenson amendments, in which they cut off both credits and trade with the Soviet Union – and when the Soviet Union became more aggressive, prevented us from resisting it. Of *course* it led to the beginning of adventures.

Then, in 1977, you had the Carter Administration, which had an absolutely wrong perception of how to deal with the Soviet Union. You remember that when Carter came in, he said he was 'free of the inordinate fear of Communism'. He certainly did nothing, to put it mildly, to arrest the collapse of the Shah of Iran. He permitted the Soviets a major adventure in the Horn of Africa. There *was* no foreign policy.

That has nothing to do with détente. *Our* policy was to resist Soviet adventurism wherever it occurred, and as long as we had any authority we managed to do this. It was not détente that produced that situation – at least not as conceived by Nixon and Ford.

CHARLTON: But would you not agree that, over Angola, the principal elements of your strategy were pretty severely tested? We find you (in October of 1976) saying that 'the introduction of Cuban expeditionary forces, with Russian support, into an area of no historic Soviet or Russian interest is totally unwarranted', and then you went on to say, 'but we've never considered SALT a favour we granted to the Soviet Union, to be turned on and off according to the ebb and flow of our relations'.

KISSINGER: Yes, but let's get a few things straight. In the fall of 1974 the Congress passed the Jackson Amendment, which cut off 'most favoured nation' treatment of the Soviets. It passed a Stevenson amendment which cut off credits. So the Soviet Union, at the end, was worse off than it had been before the détente period started. This happened at the same time, as I've said, that a McGovernite Congress had just been elected that would not support any form of resistance to Communist aggression. Then when the Soviets started stepping up their activities in Angola, and we attempted to resist, the Congress voted against the thirty million dollars we thought we needed to support the anti-Soviet and -Cuban forces (the Savimbi forces, who are still there). At that point the question was, should we cut off SALT . . . and at a time when we had a Congress that was not going to increase our military expenditures? I think it is absurd to conduct a truculent policy when you're not willing to back it up and I find myself in the ridiculous position that, in this sort of debate, I'm being attacked from the left for being too tough on the Soviets, and by the right for being too soft. We were trying to steer a middle course. Both the left and the right were trying to conduct an essentially moralistic policy – without backing it up with resources.

THE EARLY HOPES OF President Nixon and Henry Kissinger, that agreement to negotiate strategic arms limitations could be linked to Soviet assistance in America's disengagement from the sunless war in Vietnam, were not sustained. The Russians insisted that SALT was to be looked at on its own merits. With America a house divided and the uncompromising zealotry of the Communists in Hanoi, the détente policy could produce no honourable outcome in Vietnam. President Nixon's guarantees to the South Vietnamese proved not to be the bond of the American nation. Vietnam, in strategic terms, was in the end an American surrender.

HENRY KISSINGER: Certainly Vietnam was a disaster; but when you inherit a disaster, when you inherit 550,000 troops, you just cannot switch it off like a television programme. It would have been easy for Nixon, from a purely selfish point of view, to blame it all on his predecessor. But his judgment was, and I think it was correct, that the United States had no right to sacrifice 35,000 troops and simply liquidate it as if nothing had happened. After all, people forget it took de Gaulle five years to get out of Algeria.

CHARLTON: There is the evidence of what Gromyko said to Rab Butler (the British Foreign Secretary) when Butler was trying to enlist Gromyko's help about Vietnam. Gromyko said to him: 'Our American enemies are deeply embedded with men and munitions in Vietnam; we've no desire to interfere.' How much more likely is it that by 1970–71, as negotiations opened on SALT, they *did* see the American position as one of weakness?

KISSINGER: First of all, what concessions did we make to the Soviets in SALT? I mean, there is a whole series of myths that are retroactively invented which have absolutely no bearing. Can you name one concrete concession we made to the Soviets that was unwarranted – or that was not going to be imposed on us by the Congress anyway?

CHARLTON: I'm interested in how the Soviet Union saw this, and how . . .

KISSINGER: The Soviet Union, until 1971 and until our opening to China, procrastinated in negotiations. We had a number of things going for us, however. We had the opening to China. We had the fact that the Soviet Union was desperate to make an agreement with the West Germans on Berlin and East Germany, which they could not get against our active opposition. (I'm not saying it was necessary to get our *support*, but they could not get it against our active opposition.) Third, they were worried, as they always seem to be worried, by the beginning of our strategic defences.[1] And fourth, as soon as we started mining Haiphong the Soviet Union also realised that the military situation was changing. If we made a mistake, I think it was that we did not do in 1969 in Vietnam what we did in 1972 – but that would have led to a revolt in our Cabinet and Nixon was not prepared to do that.

CHARLTON: There should have been a forward policy, of mining if necessary, earlier . . . ?

KISSINGER: I believe in retrospect that we should have done in 1969 what we did in 1972: that is to say, demand a settlement, or mined the harbours and bombed North Vietnam, but then that wasn't all that easy. A bombing halt had just been signed by the outgoing administration, and by that time public order had broken down in the United States. It's very difficult for a new administration to take upon itself the responsibility for dividing the country. But, despite these difficulties, in retrospect I believe that we should have done that. In fact, I thought so at the time and recommended it. But I recommended it in a way that had no real force, nor have I ever claimed any credit for it.

CHARLTON: As you remind your critics, there was no military programme sacrificed by the Nixon–Kissinger Administration, but one still has . . .

KISSINGER: As a matter of fact, SALT, paradoxically, was the only way to *preserve* our military programmes. Without SALT the Congress would have continued to cut. Take the strategic *defence* we had at the time: it wasn't called strategic defence, it was called the anti-ballistic missile system, ABM. We started out with twelve defence sites around the country. By the time the ABM agreement was signed, the Congress had already cut it to two; in the next Budget it was going to go down to one; so the thing had become an absurdity. One defence site meant nothing. And the whole thing passed by *one* vote – the Vice-President's! Every succeeding year it went down. By 1972 it was down to two, by 1973 it would have been down to nothing.

CHARLTON: But does not this very process contribute to what it is known Brezhnev said, in Prague, at a Warsaw Pact meeting in 1973? By 1985, he said, 'as a consequence of what we are achieving through détente, we shall have achieved most of our objectives; a decisive shift in the correlation of forces will be such that we'll be able to exert our influence whenever we need to . . .'

KISSINGER: Well, first of all, I don't think he said quite that, but . . .

CHARLTON: That is what he's quoted as . . .

KISSINGER: . . . but never mind. Supposing he did say that (you have to remember that each side has the problem of justifying détente to its hardliners), the facts have certainly not borne this out. I would make the case for the proposition that détente has, on the whole, been more disarming for the Soviet Union than it has been for the West. It has brought

---

[1] i.e. the American anti-ballistic missile system, later abandoned

it endless troubles in the satellite orbit. It has not improved its relative technological position; quite the contrary, it has declined. If one looks at the growth of other nations in the Far East, it has created the problem of a two-front situation for the Soviet Union; and it led to a massive reduction in their influence in the Middle East. So, in a sense, in détente both sides were betting that they could use history. And even with an impaired Nixon, we made progress; with an unimpaired American administration, I think that situation would have been even stronger.

IN THE DYING LIGHT of the commitment in Vietnam, the American will to match limited war with limited war as a deterrent to the expansion of Communist power was, at best, uncertain. Senator Jackson pressed his attack on the consequent dangers of any perceived weakness in the central nuclear balance of power. The arithmetic of the SALT agreement had left the Russians with more offensive missiles than the Americans. But that had been the price of agreement. With or without SALT, the Russians would have had more because they were building more. What began as an arcane argument of Senator Jackson's about the theoretical possibility of a Soviet first strike against the American land-based missile force, the Minutemen, became a generalised charge that the loose constraints negotiated in SALT had presented the Russians with a claim to strategic superiority and to the political cards that go with it. An influential aide to Senator Jackson at this time, and an even more influential one today in the Reagan Administration where he is Assistant Secretary of Defence, is Richard Perle.

RICHARD PERLE: I can recall Senator Jackson sending to Henry Kissinger a memorandum in October 1970, suggesting – on the basis of intelligence that was obviously available to the Administration as well as to the Congress – that under the terms of the agreement that seemed to be emerging as the SALT I Interim Agreement the Soviets could, within the confines of that agreement (generously interpreted), double or even treble the effective capability of their land-based missile force. And that is precisely what happened.

CHARLTON: What governed your assessment of Soviet power?

PERLE: We had enjoyed a long period in which our own strategic forces were not seriously vulnerable to attack. We enjoyed that at great expense, by the development of submarine-launched ballistic missiles and the placing of land-based ballistic missiles in hardened concrete silos to shelter them from the effects of nearby nuclear blast. The inaccuracy of Soviet weapons that might be directed against those forces – all meant that a Soviet attack would fail. It would fail to destroy a significant fraction of the American retaliatory capability. For that reason there was a high degree of *stability* in the relationship.

What troubled us in the early 1970s was the prospect that the growth of Soviet forces would, in due course, lead to a situation where much of our retaliatory capability would be at risk. At the time it seemed to us that the Soviets were determined to acquire a capability to hold our retaliatory forces at risk – although this was not a proposition agreed to by the Administration. We saw the emergence of the threat which has since developed. Soviet doctrine, the structure of Soviet forces, the level of investment the Russians were then making and have continued to make since, all suggested to us that they wish to achieve a kind of military predominance which they believed (and continue to believe) translates ultimately into political power.

SENATOR HENRY JACKSON'S CRITIQUE was conditioned by a more visceral divination of the Soviet Union's intentions and capabilities, and the Senator's aide, Richard Perle, is thought to have exercised considerable persuasion over it. In his memoirs, Henry Kissinger accepted that Jackson had carefully studied Soviet tactics and strategy, and was convinced that they were out to undermine the free world. But while Kissinger agreed that this was a true enough reading of their intentions, he rejected the implication that all agreements were futile. 'Jackson objected', wrote Kissinger, 'to almost any agreement that afforded some benefits to the Soviet Union. We took it for granted that the Soviets would sign no agreement from which they did not promise themselves some gain.'

HENRY KISSINGER: I actually considered Jackson a good friend, and I agreed with many of his analyses of Soviet intentions. The difference between Jackson and me was that he wanted all-out confrontation, under the influence of one of his associates, Richard Perle. *He* wanted all-out confrontation with the Soviets, and he liked a policy of constant 'needling' of the Soviet Union. I believed that – in the face of the Vietnam War and our other pressures, and then in the face of Watergate – to court a confrontation with the Soviet Union would lead to a series of humiliations. That was one disagreement.

Secondly, I was not as pessimistic as Jackson about the evolution of the two systems. I believed that, on the whole, if we could keep the Soviet Union from expanding, we were capable of conducting a more flexible policy than the Soviet Union – as we proved in the Middle East. I did not think at all that the Soviet Union was bound to prevail in a political context. Quite the opposite.

Finally, I did not believe that the Soviet Union was gaining an advantage. It depended on whether *we* were willing to make the defence expenditures that were permitted under the agreement, and that was a matter of American decisions, not Soviet acquiescence.

THAT WAS PRECISELY THE POINT where Senator Jackson concentrated his attack on the nature of the arms control process. SALT became both an orphan and a victim when divorced from Henry Kissinger's wider context for it. 'Jackson', wrote Kissinger, 'was an absolutist who saw issues in black and white. We were gradualists seeking a policy that could be sustained over a long period.'

RICHARD PERLE: I think that is so much abstract obscurantism. Jackson believed that the only agreements worth having were agreements that diminished the magnitude of the threat we faced. Agreements that *permitted* the threat faced by the United States and its allies were not worth having. That is precisely the sort of agreement that was achieved in 1972. Since the opening rounds of the discussions that led to the agreement in 1972, the Soviets have added more than 8000 strategic warheads to their inventory. The threat has increased enormously. It was the *quality* of the agreement and not the fact of the agreement to which we took exception.

CHARLTON: Henry Kissinger maintains that he did not believe the Soviet Union *was* gaining an advantage. It depended, he said 'on whether we were willing to make the defence expenditures permitted under the agreement, and that was a matter of American decisions, not Soviet acquiescence.'

PERLE: It's fair to ask what was the point of arms control that set the stage for a requirement that we make massive additional investments in precisely the strategic arms that were the subject of the negotiation, while permitting the Soviets also to make massive investment in additional strategic forces. That was the point about the failure of the Interim Agreement. It permitted very sizeable growth on both sides. In my view it didn't restrain the Soviet Union at all, in any significant way.

CHARLTON: But when you and Jackson drafted the ratification of SALT I (and the Jackson Amendment), Kissinger appears to have taken the view that your attack was fundamental. It caught him unawares. 'They sought to destroy our policy', he has said, 'not to ameliorate it.'

PERLE: No, the reality was that the Interim Agreement was going to pass the Senate. There was no doubt in our minds about that. So we sought instead to condition, or attempt to condition, future agreements. The Jackson Amendment says simply that future agreements must be on the basis of equality – because the 1972 agreement clearly was not.

CHARLTON: Do you take the view that equality can be established as a fact? Because if it can't, isn't that tantamount to saying that no agreement is possible?

PERLE: I think equality can be established as a fact, but I think it is very difficult to freeze equality. The strategic forces of both sides are in a constant state of flux and evolution. And as vulnerabilities are discovered, they need to be fixed; as imbalances develop they need to be corrected. The role of arms control in accomplishing that is a much more difficult proposition.

Looking back on 1972, I think Henry Kissinger would have a hard time arguing that that agreement facilitated our maintenance of an effective balance. Indeed, in discussions I've had with him, he lays great stress not on the military benefits of the 1972 agreement but on the political necessity as he saw it at the time. With the emotions of Vietnam affecting the American Congress and public as profoundly as they then did affect us, he wanted to buy a bit of time in which we might regroup, in order more effectively to compete with the Soviet Union.

THE INFERENCE THAT HENRY KISSINGER's détente policy embodied a melancholy pessimism about the American will to sustain a policy of containment became central to the political debate which led, in the end, to the Reagan Presidency. The critics of SALT questioned the assumption that the Soviet Union could be contained other than by American power. As Kissinger said, it was part of a larger controversy over whether arms control enhanced or weakened the security of the West.

Kissinger himself rejected the notion which appeared in the anti-ballistic missile debate (as it had in the debate over the hydrogen bomb in the 1950s), that unilateral restraint by the United States would induce the Russians to follow suit. There was, he said, overwhelming evidence to the contrary.

Early in the Nixon Administration, in the new uncertainties created by the Soviet invasion of Czechoslovakia, and following the domestic upheavals over the course of the Vietnam War which caused President Johnson to step aside, the Americans had taken the decision to go ahead and be the first to *deploy* the multiple-warhead missile, MIRV. The decision was criticised at the time and – almost more than any other since – has been held responsible for making a huge increase in the nuclear arsenals of both sides inevitable. Research and development of MIRV was begun in the previous administration, as Robert McNamara reminded us earlier, 'solely as a means of countering the Soviet deployment of an anti-ballistic missile defence'.

HENRY KISSINGER: Secretary McNamara did not want to build an anti-ballistic missile defence. He therefore developed the idea of a MIRV, arguing that with MIRV we could saturate any Soviet defence and that therefore there would be no strategic inequality if the Soviets had a defensive system and we did not. By the time the Nixon Administration came into office in 1969, more than ten tests of MIRVs had already been conducted. It is generally thought that weapons are operational at a maximum of twenty tests, but certainly, by the time you have undertaken ten tests you have gone down the road toward proving the weapon. Then, for a while, the Soviets were reluctant to enter negotiations.

So by November 1969 (when negotiations started), probably fifteen tests had been conducted on a schedule established by the previous administration. Most of its members then started opposing – just as they had with the Vietnam War – what they themselves had created. We had no assurance *at all* that the Soviets would agree to a limitation of ballistic missile defences. We in fact proposed, and we opened, the MIRV discussion – admittedly with an unacceptable proposal. The proposal was that there should be a stoppage of all testing. The Soviets countered with a proposal that there should be a stoppage of all *deployment*, but that *testing* should be permitted. Of course, this was an easy way for them to catch up.

CHARLTON: Rather like the SDI issue now?

KISSINGER: Right. So that is where it stalemated. Now, should we also have proposed, at that point, that there should be a stop to *both* testing and deployment? Well, this is a tactical issue. Historical experience with the Soviets shows that, if they wanted an agreement limiting MIRVs, we could not have driven them off the table with it. They would have deluged us with it. Our primary problem at that point was to keep enough support for the agreements that we *were* making, and MIRV was the one programme that the Defence Department had that was not being contested in any significant way – or any decisive way – by the Congress.

As soon as we had the SALT I agreement, we made a whole series of proposals on MIRVs to the Soviet Union which would have imposed severe limitations – none of which they accepted. So, should we have made it two years earlier? It's easy to say in the light of all that happened. One always has to consider the option in any one field compared to the totality of issues that were before us.

CHARLTON: In December 1974 you said, of MIRV, that it was the same question people faced when the H-bomb was developed. It raises the issue whether it's the United States development which then in turn produces that same development on the other side.

KISSINGER: And I think the answer is the same. The Soviets started deploying MIRVs in 1973, which means that they were well along by 1970 and 1971, which is the time we may have had an opportunity. As it turned out, we exploded our H-bomb about nine months before the Soviets. We deployed our MIRVs about eighteen months before the Soviets. It is impossible therefore that they could have developed MIRVs just in that short interval *between* the time we did and they did.

MIRV AND ITS FRATRICIDAL counterpart ABM, the anti-ballistic missile, were respectively offence and defence, sword and shield. Superficially they had transported this classical antithesis into the nuclear era. But given the enormous power of even a single nuclear weapon, the ancient discord of sword and shield were adjudged unconvincing by Robert McNamara. It fell to Henry Kissinger to search for some common understanding of the proposition that, in the nuclear age, the adversary becomes in a sense a partner in the avoidance of nuclear war as a political and moral necessity.

The historic essence of the first SALT agreement, the Anti-Ballistic Missile Treaty of 1972, was that each side renounced the defence of its society against the nuclear arsenal of the other. As Henry Kissinger has reminded us, the US Congress had cut the budgets for an American counterpart to the already deployed Soviet ABM defence system 'to an absurdity'. But in the labyrinth of the SALT accord is Ariadne's thread – which leads us, in the present day, to President Reagan's case for the 'Star Wars' defence.

Two expectations arising from SALT I were not fulfilled. Henry Kissinger had hoped to shape the outcome so as to delay the trend which would give the Soviet Union a first-strike capability against the American land-based missiles by the 1980s, and then to use that delay to negotiate reductions in the numbers of offensive missiles in another and more comprehensive agreement. But the speed and extent to which the Soviet Union built up their offensive forces were underestimated.

HENRY KISSINGER: You have to understand a number of things about the Anti-Ballistic Missile Treaty. First, there are a great many heroes *now* who were in their foxholes when all this was going on! At the time of the Anti-Ballistic Missile Treaty, the number of US missile sites, as I've already pointed out, had been reduced to two. So our choice was whether we were going to agree to the Congress unilaterally dismantling the anti-ballistic missile defences, or whether we were going to get something for it from the Soviet Union.

At that time the build-up of Soviet offensive forces was in its infancy. We made a unilateral statement (or we had our delegation make a unilateral statement) to read into the record that the United States considered the continued existence of the Anti-Ballistic Missile Treaty to depend on significant *cuts* in offensive forces. If these offensive forces were not reduced within the time limit of the offensive agreement, then the conditions for abrogation of the treaty would exist.

Rather than this leading to a reduction of offensive forces, the Soviets built up their offensive forces to a remarkable degree. So the balance between offensive and defensive forces was substantially destroyed. As soon as the ABM treaty and SALT I were signed, we initiated negotiations for the limitation of multiple warheads and reductions to very small numbers. *That* the Soviets consistently refused. So we have a totally new situation today.

DR KISSINGER REMAINS CONVINCED, however, that SALT was made, in his words, 'the whipping boy' for a more fundamental philosophical contest in East-West relations. The extent to which American strategic policy should be informed by a discussion of 'moral principles' rather than assembled for 'great practical purposes' (the distinction Castlereagh made concerning the Congress of Vienna), and the extent to which it was a reflection of domestic impulses and emotions – therefore subjective rather than objective – could not be resolved. That same Soviet Union with which, in President Nixon's Administration, Kissinger established a wide range of contacts, is the one with which President Reagan much later would find it difficult to collaborate at all – for essentially the reasons given by Senator Jackson's associate (and now President Reagan's Assistant Secretary for Defence) Richard Perle.

RICHARD PERLE: The kind of business that was done in 1972 was profitable, but profitable for one side only. The Soviets will always be prepared to do business with us if it produces an advantage for the Soviet Union. I haven't the slightest doubt that Mr Gorbachev would cheerfully sign agreements with the United States that accomplish for him what the 1972 agreement accomplished for Brezhnev.

Look at the other agreements of that period. I don't think one can take the arms control agreements in isolation. There was an agreement on grain which led immediately to a massive Soviet raid on the American grain harvest, pushing up the price of grain to American consumers and solving a very serious Soviet problem. There were agreements on science and technology that led to very significant transfers of technology to the Soviet Union, and we now see them showing up in Soviet military systems. There was a general agreement on principles governing the relationship that crowned a thirty-year Soviet effort to induce the West to accept the principles contained in that document – the Soviet policy line of 'peaceful co-existence' and the like. I think, looking back on that period, that the agreements signed were in every case advantageous to the Soviet Union, and I think that's all one needs to know in order to explain their readiness to sign them.

NEITHER HENRY KISSINGER NOR PRESIDENT NIXON had any desire to accommodate their critics. To a large extent they shared the philosophical case against the Soviet state and its ideology. Dr Kissinger thought of Senator Jackson as an ally and regretted that the Senator chose to oppose him. It was, wrote Kissinger in his memoirs, 'a national tragedy that those who shared a similar strategic analysis should conduct a civil war over tactics . . .'

But the gap was surely wider than a disagreement over tactics. Both sides wished to 'contain' the Soviet Union. Kissinger thought that, with seductive inducements, the Soviet Union might be escorted from its traditional expansionism to restraint, and that Russia's economic failures and fear over Kissinger's bringing China into play would press the Soviet leaders to co-existence on the West's terms. The other side – Kissinger's conservative opponents – saw nothing but an implacable adversary and an endless vista of contests and confrontations. At that well-remembered press conference in Moscow in 1974, Henry Kissinger asked a question that has often been quoted since: '*What in the name of God is strategic superiority?*' The resonance of this has been sustained. How should the historian understand him?

HENRY KISSINGER: That is absolutely correct. I do not believe that you can rely on a first-strike strategy as the defence against all contingencies. Again, one has to consider this in the context of events. That remark was made in early July 1974 in Moscow, a month before Nixon was forced out of office. We found ourselves in the position of being harassed on détente at a time when we had absolutely no capacity for confrontation. And I still believe this: I do not think it is possible to achieve the degree of strategic superiority that existed in the 1940s and 1950s, such that we can rely on nuclear superiority to defend Europe and other parts of the world. I remind you that Reagan has never tired of pointing out in the last two or three years that we are not trying to win a war. In what way does that differ from what I said ten years earlier?

CHARLTON: One of your most persistent and formidable critics, Senator Jackson, sought to know why you had not demanded lower limits from the Soviet Union, as he felt you should have. I thought you gave a very interesting answer to that on the way to Peking in 1974, which was taken down verbatim at the time. I'd like to read it to you. You said:

> The only way we could even have talked about lower numbers was to drastically increase defence spending and to hold the increase for a number of years, long enough to convince the Soviets that we were going to drive the race through the ceiling with them . . .

That sounds very like the Reagan programme today.

KISSINGER: Exactly correct. That is still my view.

DR HENRY KISSINGER'S HAND WAS EVERYWHERE during one of the most creative periods in post-war diplomacy, of which he is one of the great public figures. Why did he think disenchantment with détente set in so early? 'Overall,' Kissinger says, détente was 'ground down between a liberal idealism unrelated to a concept of power and the liturgical anti-Communism of the right'. But, Kissinger has said, although we made our share of mistakes, the fundamental assault on détente was made by the Soviet Union: with the Soviet-Cuban expeditionary forces in Angola and Ethiopia; their appearance in Aden; the Kremlin's encouragement of North Vietnam's takeover of the South; the pressures on Poland; and the invasion of Afghanistan. Détente had not deterred.

Over the next few years and during the long agony for détente of the Carter Presidency, the strategic debate in the United States was powerfully shaped by forces associated with the Committee on the Present Danger. They would return a different answer to Henry Kissinger's question in Moscow that July night in 1974: 'What in the name of God is strategic superiority?'

3

RED ALERT:

Paul Nitze and the Present Danger

THE IMPEACHMENT OF PRESIDENT NIXON, and the annihilating victory of North Vietnam over the South in 1975, crowned the political defeat of the United States. The American body politic fell into a numbing and troubled introspection. It was a 'dark night of the soul' for Thomas Jefferson's Republic. When it came to President Nixon and Henry Kissinger's choice and conduct of a policy of détente – designed to mitigate the ambitions of the Soviet Union – the reasonable logic of 'what might have been' was slowly replaced by the more passionate logic of what had actually happened.

The predominance of the United States, which had continued to guarantee the appearance of order since the end of World War II, belonged to the past. As the Vietnam War had dragged on, neither public opinion nor the Congress would vote the money for an accelerated arms race whose objective was superiority. In SALT I (the first agreement to limit strategic weapons signed by Nixon and Brezhnev in 1972), the Americans formally acknowledged their acceptance of the Soviet Union's achievement of nuclear parity. Both sides renounced an area defence of their overall territory and populations against nuclear attack. However, the Soviet Union maintained its deployment of an anti-ballistic missile system around Moscow, while the Americans did not exercise a similar option for Washington.

SALT I left the Americans with a greater number of nuclear warheads, and the Soviet Union with their larger, and so more powerful, missiles. Mr Brezhnev had said it was warheads that kill, not missiles, but any American President was bound to point out that, as the Russians placed more and more warheads on their larger rockets, the Soviet Union would have an overall superiority in these offensive arms that challenged the American notion of stability. In other words, both sides had subscribed to a parity which, in the absence of follow-on agreements, would be transient.

If the use of nuclear weapons guaranteed mutual destruction, then, arising out of that nuclear stalemate, it was *conventional* military power which shaped the outcome. And, if a great power used conventional superiority to harm a rival great power's vital interests, it would violate the unspoken assumptions of arms control. This, essentially, was the challenge to nuclear deterrence, in part created and starkly posed following the American disaster in Vietnam.

Over the next few years the American strategic debate was powerfully influenced, both in and out of government, by those Americans who formed the Committee on the Present Danger. Foremost among them was Paul Nitze, who is now President Reagan's chief arms negotiator. He had been 'present at the creation', as it were, as head of Policy Planning in the State Department (he succeeded George Kennan) in the early years after World War II, when America's fundamental post-war commitments and alliances were being formed. Nitze has held high responsibility for strategic matters in almost every American administration since the end of the war, and in the latter half of the 1970s he largely fashioned the character of the nuclear arms debate in America.

PAUL NITZE: Some of us in 1975, 1976, 1977 came to the conclusion that there was an inadequate understanding of the degree to which a combination of a regime which continued to believe in the Marxist-Leninist objectives and which was building a superior military capability would exploit that military capability – not necessarily in *military* terms, but in political terms around the world, bit by bit, chip by chip, incident by incident.

CHARLTON: What Kennedy called, I think, being 'nibbled to death in a nuclear stalemate'?

NITZE: Exactly. Yes, exactly that. This was not widely recognised. It was necessary to emphasise it; there were so many voices which were taking the opposite point of view, this 'arms race' point of view. I think Paul Warnke[1] was the leading one who used the analogy of two apes on a treadmill: that they were competing, and if one of the apes would get off, the situation would be cured. In other words, the whole reason for the 'arms race' was the fact that the United States had not ceased its efforts to deny the Soviet Union a useful military superiority. I thought that was a very dangerous deviation from common-sense thinking, and so did some of my friends.

CHARLTON: Why did you decide that the Soviet Union's underlying motive was to gain a position of superiority?

NITZE: Because close examination of all the facts led me to that view, and it continues to lead me to that view. I do not believe that those who took a different view of the facts are sustained by what has happened since. We

[1] Director of US Arms Control and Disarmament Agency 1977–78 and chief SALT negotiator in Carter Administration

had a considerable debate – a battle – over the ratification or non-ratification of SALT II. I put out a long series of detailed statistics, with all the information which lay behind those statistics. Everybody laughed at those and said, you know, 'Paul is smoking pot!' or 'Why does he raise this now?'. But I believe that if you look now at those statistics, they're better than anybody else's predictions from that time on, because they projected what the force relationships would be up to 1985 and, if anything, they were conservative. I repeat the point: it makes a difference whether you look at the facts and try to look at them with open eyes. If you're just looking at *words* you get into trouble. You're much better off looking at the *facts*.

FOR PAUL NITZE AND his fellow members of the Committee on the Present Danger, the ultimate issue of East-West relations was defined in the nuclear arms talks. There, the nuclear weapon was held to be the master of all its interlocutors. But did it in fact impose a common moderation? More particularly, did the Soviet Union still believe that its salvationist mission on earth was to spread the true faith by the sword and subversion?

There was no universal American opinion, and Nitze and his friends set out to appeal across Democratic-Republican party lines. Among those friends was another distinguished Democrat. He had served in the administrations of three Democratic Presidents: Roosevelt, Truman and Johnson; and a fourth President, the Republican Ronald Reagan, would appoint him to the post Paul Warnke had held as head of the Arms Control and Disarmament Agency. For several years he chaired the Executive Committee of the Committee on the Present Danger. Like Nitze, Eugene Rostow sought the refreshment of America – following constitutional crisis, and defeat in war – in the former certainties of the era of containment.

EUGENE ROSTOW: We had formed a committee within the Democratic Party to try to rally the faithful to the traditional policy of the party since the time of Roosevelt and Truman. It didn't gain much headway, and therefore we decided to form a bipartisan committee, which is a very characteristic thing for Americans to do when they want to press a cause. We waited until after the election of 1976, but we prepared for it. And the reason underlying all this was, of course, the weakening of the support for the *bipartisan* foreign policy of Truman and Acheson ... the policy occasioned first by Korea, and then most acutely by Vietnam and by the tragic experience of failure in Vietnam. So this was to say to the American people: well, Vietnam was a failure, but *there is no other policy*, and we must rally public opinion to realise that we've lost a battle and not the war, and that the protection of the national interests of the United States requires that kind of a policy – a policy of *collective* security.

CHARLTON: There was another Committee on the Present Danger at the time of the Korean War, and I wonder if you meant it to have, in the 1970s, the particular resonance that the Korean War had in the 1950s, in calling for rearmament?

ROSTOW: Exactly. Calling for rearmament and a strengthening of the policy of solidarity. Trying to repair the damage which had been done to the national foreign policy consensus by Vietnam.

CHARLTON: No doubt there were many ingredients in the making of your decision, but what was the final spur to forming the Committee on the Present Danger?

ROSTOW: The final spur was the sense that we had very little time; that the hopes that had been invested in SALT I, and in Nixon's policy of détente, were manifestly proving to be false; and that the Soviets were gaining so rapidly in nuclear strength, despite the provisions of SALT I and the prospective provisions of SALT II, that we soon would have no alternative but to surrender. The Soviet policy with regard to nuclear weapons and therefore with regard to arms control agreements was extremely astute and well conceived; but it was a policy not of détente, not of relaxation of tensions, but of nuclear blackmail.

EUGENE ROSTOW'S PERCEPTIONS of the Soviet Union were those which had been broadly endorsed by the Americans during the period of the Cold War. It was central to the crusade of the Committee on the Present Danger that events had once more shown the Soviet Union to be incorrigibly militant. The hopes nurtured by the activity called 'détente', and the process of arms control conducted by Henry Kissinger, stood, by these lights, confounded.

The basic concept of parity in the SALT negotiations, as an acceptable strategic relationship with the Soviet Union, was attacked as placing the United States at a disadvantage. While the United States adhered to deterrence and retaliation, parity – plus the Soviet policy of strategic initiative (a belief in a first strike, and weapons assigned with that use in mind) – in fact gave the Russians *superiority*.

This critique was put forward in answer to Henry Kissinger's much-quoted question, uttered in Moscow in July 1974: 'What in the name of God is strategic superiority?' The claim that the SALT talks had acquiesced in an American disadvantage and that Kissinger's approach was fatally flawed is, naturally, in conflict with the views of Henry Kissinger himself, particularly concerning the 'quality' of the SALT I Interim Agreement – the target of what would become the prevailing indictment of détente.

HENRY KISSINGER: At the time of the Interim Agreement, the Soviets were building about 240 missiles a year, and we were building none. We considered it a considerable achievement that we were stopping the build-up of Soviet forces. Now, of course, you can say that the Soviets would have stopped anyway. Nobody can ever prove that. We thought the

maximum we could achieve in 1972 was to get a freeze on the *additional*
'digging of holes' or of silos by the Soviet Union. Our strategy then was
that, in the next period, we were going to strive for a *reduction* of these,
plus a reduction of warheads. What we could have achieved if there had
not been any Watergate, nobody can ever know.

The fact is that as soon as the agreement was signed, suddenly people
started saying this sanctified an inequality of numbers – which was total
nonsense, *because they did not count the bombers*. They just counted the
missiles. They did not count the fact that we had multiple warheads, that
they did not. We then achieved – even after Watergate, under President
Ford – equality in numbers. Whereupon the debate shifted on to the
'Backfire' bomber, which has since disappeared from the scene. The basic
difficulty is that if you have an opposition that is determined to wreck
any negotiation on a subject as technologically complicated as SALT, the
administration in office is in an almost hopeless position.

CHARLTON: In fact, Admiral Moorer, the Chairman of the Joint Chiefs of
Staff at the time, giving evidence about this, said the SALT I treaty should
be seen not in the light of what it had frozen but of what it had
forestalled. That you had actually forestalled what would by 1977 have
been a three-to-two ratio in the Soviet Union's favour.

KISSINGER: That's exactly correct.

CHARLTON: Nonetheless, we find Paul Nitze saying by the mid-1970s
that the Soviets were not following a strategy of deterrence and
retaliation: 'They spelled out their belief in a strategy of first strike' and
their weapons had been assigned 'with that in mind'. Therefore, in their
case, 'Parity plus their policy of "strategic initiative" gives them
superiority.'

KISSINGER: Well, there are a number of things . . . I think Nitze is a man
of considerable knowledge and one of the most experienced people we
have in this field. He felt badly treated by Nixon – and by me I suppose –
at the time of the Moscow signing, and there was some merit in it . . .

CHARLTON: In what respect?

KISSINGER: In the sense that the delegation had done ninety-five per cent
of the negotiating in Helsinki and Nixon took one hundred per cent of
the credit in Moscow. On the other hand, that is not unusual. That is
what Presidents tend to do, and in an ultimate sense it is their
prerogative. You don't expect laurels to be given to the individual
negotiators. (On the other hand, they were not treated well. They were
treated rudely and I've pointed that out.)

I do not believe that the Soviets are relying on a first strike. I *do* believe
that the Soviet Union has designed its strategic forces with a more
military concept than the United States has. They do have the capacity to
prevent a tit-for-tat, because they can respond with more military options
than we can. In other words, they can force us into initiating the
destruction of civilian targets earlier than *they* have to. That gives them a

great advantage – not to wipe out our retaliatory forces, though they may be able to do that to our *land-based* retaliatory force.

CHARLTON: What is your response, then, to a SALT critic like Paul Nitze, who said that the basic concept of parity was the flaw for him in the SALT agreements, because parity can't be precisely determined and it puts the United States at a disadvantage because of the differences in military strategy?

KISSINGER: First of all, you've never heard Nitze say anything like that when he was in a position of responsibility. You've only heard Nitze say that out of office; you haven't heard him say that in office. And neither in our administration, nor in the administration he is serving now, has he ever taken anything like that position. On the contrary, he has been more on the conciliatory side – conciliatory in the sense of trying to find something in the point of view that could be negotiated.

CHARLTON: More inclined to 'walk in the woods'?

KISSINGER: Exactly. That's right. And now with the Strategic Defence Initiative he has stated criteria that are in fact unfulfillable, so that operationally he is working more in that direction. But the option of superiority did not exist at the time. There was no programme that we could get through the Congress. There is no programme that we *stopped* in the Nixon Administration.

It is true that we probably underestimated the speed with which the Soviet Union would 'MIRV'. But by the year 1984 that does not make any difference. The strategic gains the Soviets had made were not due to the rapidity of their 'MIRVing', but due to the irresolution of the Carter Administration. Supposing the Soviets had 'MIRVed' more slowly? We would still have lost Iran. We still would have had a Sandinista government in Nicaragua.

CHARLTON: Yet there is this division still, isn't there, over these perceptions of power which the central nuclear balance conveys. Between those who say the Nicaraguas and Angolas are assisted into history because the central nuclear balance has altered . . . that Khruschev withdrew from Cuba because of that ultimate reality, American strategic superiority, and . . .

KISSINGER: No. Khruschev withdrew from Cuba because we had *local* superiority. On top of it, what made it easier was that we also had strategic superiority. We could easily have handled Angola if the Congress had not cut our forces. Whether we could have handled Iran or not can be debated for ever, but certainly – even if we had had superiority – we would not have threatened to use nuclear weapons against the Soviet Union in order to keep Khomeini from coming to power. We surely would not have used nuclear weapons to keep the Sandinistas from coming to power, since *we put* them into power – and that had nothing to do with the strategic balance. That had to do with the understanding of pure political reality.

CHARLTON: You've written of the period of the decline of détente and of support for arms control that its critics were clamouring 'for a course whose practical consequence was to elevate confrontation into a principle of policy . . .'

KISSINGER: Yes, but without being willing to pay the price for it.

CHARLTON: '. . . in the middle of the worst domestic crisis in a century'.

KISSINGER: And, I repeat, without being willing to pay any price. They thought that if you blow the trumpet hard enough the walls of Jericho were going to collapse automatically.

THE SITUATION WITH WHICH Kissinger had been confronted was the one which Nitze and his associates campaigned to redress. Whereas Kissinger had sought to transcend the ideological differences in the co-operative entanglements of détente, the Committee on the Present Danger examined the Soviet challenge much more in terms of the ideological concepts which the Soviet leadership used to describe and defend their policies.

The principal formulation of American strategic policy during the era of containment of Soviet power, which began under President Truman, was a document known as NSC (National Security Council) 68. Then, as now, the military strength of the West was held to be dangerously inadequate. NSC 68 considered the Soviet design of world domination to be indivisible from the Communist system and fatal to the West. The Soviet Union, the inheritor of Russian imperialism, possessed and was possessed by a worldwide revolutionary movement which *required* the dynamic extension of its authority. The author of NSC 68, adopted by President Truman as policy when North Korea (aided by Soviet Russia) invaded South Korea in 1950, was Paul Nitze.

PAUL NITZE: If I might say a word about the origin of it. This was at a time when we found out that the Soviets had tested an atomic weapon in 1949. It was also right after Chiang Kai-Shek had been driven from the mainland of China. I'd been much impressed by a book written by a man called Nathan Leites, who talked about the 'standard operating code' of the Kremlin. In it he stressed the fact that when the 'correlation of forces' was unfavourable, Lenin had adopted the doctrine that that was a time when one ought to throw dust into the enemy's eyes, so that one would have time to rebuild and to change the correlation of forces. So these two events, the removal of our monopoly and the consolidation of Communist control over the mainland, would be two radical changes in the correlation of forces which the Soviets were bound to take into account if they were still following the precepts that Lenin had laid down.

CHARLTON: As in Lenin's famous remark: 'Probe with bayonets, and if you strike mush, go on – if you meet resistance, retreat.'

NITZE: That's correct. Up to that time, US policy and Allied policy generally had been emphasising entirely the economic and the political elements of policy and had paid little attention to the military aspects. Our defence budget was twelve-and-a-half billion dollars, and the European defence budgets were very small – and should have been small – because they were concentrating on economic recovery.

CHARLTON: When you wrote NSC 68, how much confidence did you personally feel, how much did you express, that the two great nuclear powers could exist 'mutually deterred' in a stable relationship?

NITZE: We felt really quite confident that it could be done. But it required many things which were quite different from a world in which only one power had nuclear weapons. In a world where one power, the United States, which was a democratic country and a member of an alliance of democratic countries – if that power had nuclear weapons, then there was no danger that nuclear weapons could get out of hand. Because a democracy and an alliance of democracies would not permit, really, a democratic country to use those nuclear weapons except under the most extreme conditions of provocation.

CHARLTON: Therefore, what view did NSC 68 take of the relative advantages enjoyed by a totalitarian state that had nuclear weapons, compared with the open society which had nuclear weapons?

NITZE: That – thank goodness – the totalitarian state would not have a monopoly. We had *had* a monopoly. We used that monopoly with great restraint, I think, very wisely. But the problem was what would happen when there were two countries which had nuclear weapons – one of them a *totalitarian* state. It seemed to us to be clear that, over time, the Soviets would develop their nuclear capability more and more; and that, even if we did our best to maintain ours, the margin of advantage we could maintain would decrease over the years to the point where it would cease to be of much use politically. Therefore, one of the conclusions of NSC 68 was that we ought to place increasing attention upon *conventional* military capabilities.

CHARLTON: You've just said that you felt confident that two powers possessing the atomic weapon could co-exist in some sort of mutually stable relationship. But my own reading of NSC 68 was that you had very *little* confidence in that. You foresaw the danger of war not just from accident or from crisis, or accident arising out of crisis, but from a premeditated Russian aggression.

NITZE: Well, we felt that the Marxist-Leninist doctrine did dedicate itself to a world which would be completely Socialist as a transitional stage to the worldwide triumph of Communism, and that this called for every effort by the Soviet Union to promote such a world. NSC 68 did say, however, that the primary objective of the Communist Party in the Soviet Union was to maintain control over the Soviet Union: that the second objective was to maintain control over the associated states (the satellites, as we called them in those days); and that a third objective was to do what it could to promote the worldwide triumph of Communism. So it wasn't a first but a third objective. Still, that was a very *real* objective in our view.

When it came to the means that they would use, we had long thought they would use every means – political, economic and subversive. The question at issue in NSC 68 was, would they now use *military* means with (from their standpoint) this improvement in the correlation of forces? We thought they might. We thought they would try to do it through satellites if possible, rather than directly. But still, they might very well do it.

CHARLTON: I have here something which you wrote (an article for *Foreign Affairs* in 1956) in which you stated your belief, some six years after NSC 68, that the West should maintain indefinitely a position of nuclear attack and defence superiority versus the Soviet Union and its satellites. Where does that belief stand in your own mind now?

NITZE: I argued then that that was not only a 'should' proposition, but a 'could' proposition. The circumstances were such that there was no reason why we could not do it, provided the Alliance held together and the Alliance, as a whole, had certain geographical advantages over the Soviet Union. We did, in fact: the members of the Alliance controlled much of the periphery, and the oceans of the world. So we really should be able to maintain control of the seas – the waters under them and the air above – and the periphery of the Eurasian landmass. As a result of that we would have advantages which could give us a degree of superiority over the long-range future.

Today the situation is such that this is no longer a feasible proposition. The Soviets have developed certain advantages in what is called 'prompt hard-target kill capability' – in fact, distinct advantages over the West in that sphere. They've also developed certain other advantages: they have the only defence against nuclear ballistic missiles today, they have the only operational anti-satellite system, and they have a distinct advantage in conventional weapons on the Eurasian landmass.

CHARLTON: So how have you tried to influence the debate once parity, or an equivalent Soviet nuclear capability, became established? As one who, clearly, was convinced that the West had no alternative, given its inferiority in conventional weapons, but to attach a special significance to nuclear weapons – what view have you taken of the acceptance of nuclear stalemate?

NITZE: I have not thought it wise to accept nuclear stalemate because that is tantamount, really, to accepting nuclear inferiority. At least one must strive for a situation in which one can deny the other side superiority. Perhaps you can argue that that is stalemate. I would argue that it is not.

CHARLTON: Well, from what you've just said, it seems to me that you've never really abandoned the belief that lay at the heart of NSC 68, as you sat down to write it for the 1950s. Is that a fair assessment of your position? Let me quote it to you once more: 'The West should maintain indefinitely a position of nuclear attack and defence superiority versus the Soviet Union and its satellites'.

NITZE: Today I do not believe it is possible. I do believe that it is possible to deny the Soviet Union a *usable* superiority – and I think everybody in the West ought to be unified on that objective. I think the world would be better off, you know, if the West *had* superiority. I have no doubt of that in my mind. I do not believe it is possible to have equal forces on both sides. I think ours are less than the Soviets, and will continue to be less, because a coalition of democracies will not *permit* us to build up to the full level the Soviets have. Not that it would not be desirable for us to have more – but the coalition of democracies won't let that be done.

IN THE FIRST YEARS AFTER Nixon's downfall – while President Ford and later President Carter were endeavouring to consummate the SALT process which Kissinger had woven into the fabric of détente – the Committee on the Present Danger was making an increasingly effective public utterance. Nitze and his associates distilled the Byzantine complexities of SALT to a simple essence: the Soviet leaders had succeeded in making the state of the military balance a powerful political influence, and this was, as Eugene Rostow saw it, 'the source of currents of fear which were transforming political positions all across the spectrum of Western politics'.

EUGENE ROSTOW: The nuclear balance was changing, and changing very rapidly – which meant that the credibility of the American guarantees to Europe, to Japan, to South Korea (guarantees that were less formal but were obvious in the political situation, guarantees to protect our vital military interests) were losing their credibility. General de Gaulle said it for the first time; Henry Kissinger said it over and over again; and a great many other people were beginning to believe it, even though they did not say it out loud in public.
CHARLTON: You're thinking of Kissinger's speech in Brussels where he said, 'You cannot go on expecting us to multiply assurances we cannot possibly mean . . .'?
ROSTOW: No, he said something else. He said, 'Great powers don't commit suicide for their allies.' It was a very blunt and very brutal (and, I think, in the circumstances profoundly unwise) statement. We saw the change in the nuclear balance, the sudden and very rapid increase in Soviet nuclear strength – especially in the field of ground-based ballistic missiles – as a threat to deterrence.
CHARLTON: But you part company with those who see the nuclear weapon as having no utility other than to deter other people from using them?
ROSTOW: Absolutely. I think the heart of the problem is that we in the West find it very difficult to believe that the Soviet theory about nuclear weapons is not the same as our own. And I think that now, in 1985, if you look back at what's happened, and especially at the huge build-up of the Soviet nuclear force since 1972 (the date of the first SALT agreement), you've got to accept that the Western view of the function of nuclear

weapons, *and therefore the function of the arms control agreements*, is entirely different from the Soviet view. We are looking to assure stability and to remove the causes of accidental war; they are seeking nuclear superiority and our acceptance of their right to nuclear superiority, so as to assure American neutrality. Henry Kissinger asked that famous question, 'What on earth can you do with nuclear superiority?' I think the Soviets have a very clear answer, and it's now obvious. Their theory of building a huge nuclear force was not to have a nuclear war, but it was exactly the theory of the Kaiser before 1914, who built a huge fleet not to fight the Royal Navy but to assure British neutrality in the event of a continental war. And what the Soviets are trying to do is to assure American neutrality in the event of a war either in the Pacific or in the Atlantic.

ROSTOW'S CONCLUSION ABOUT Soviet intentions and capabilities echoed those of Truman and Acheson in the era of containment. It called up spirits from the vast deep of the Cold War. And the question Shakespeare had Hotspur ask of Glendower – 'But will they come when you do call for them?' – became the issue in the American strategic debate, and was put to the proof of public opinion.

It was the achievement of this remarkably energetic set of foreign policy advisers who formed the Committee on the Present Danger – for both Eugene Rostow and Paul Nitze were men in their seventies – that they showed themselves to be the triumphal branch of that debate. It undermined the efforts of Henry Kissinger and President Ford, and later President Carter, to have ratified a second SALT accord. It also paved the way for President Reagan to summon up the old spirit of containment of the 1950s, and win public support for its corollary – greatly increased spending on defence.

The early claims of the Nixon Administration for the Anti-Ballistic Missile Treaty, which was the cornerstone of arms control, did little to discourage the notion that the two rival political systems, in their concepts arising from the nuclear reality, had converged in a significant way. But Nitze, who was one of the chief negotiators of SALT I, is vehemently sceptical on this point. And the history of the Committee on the Present Danger suggests that it particularly influenced public attitudes when deep concern was allied with deep knowledge – and, as in Nitze's case, long experience. It was on the advice and with the support of Nitze that Robert McNamara had initiated the process, in the late 1960s, which ended in the SALT I and ABM agreements.

PAUL NITZE: I had been for arms control, if one could do it, for a long time. President Kennedy had asked me to devote most of my time to arms control in 1961 when I became Assistant Secretary of Defence. I think in that part of the Pentagon we had the leading role in doing the work which led, for instance, to the Limited Test Ban Treaty, the Non-Proliferation

Treaty, the Outer Space Treaty – and we had also done the initial study on the issues involved in bilateral negotiations with the Soviet Union on strategic nuclear weapons. Even before that, in 1959 and 1960, I'd been an adviser to our delegation at the five-nation disarmament conference in Geneva. I've been in this business as long as you can remember! So that this wasn't just a bolt out of the blue that somebody, suddenly, thought of arms control. Arms control has, ever since 1946, always been an element which has been important in US policy. The question at issue has been whether or not it is practical; whether or not one can, in fact, get useful arms control which will contribute to a reduction in the risk of war.

CHARLTON: Would you find any serious quarrel with something that Dr Herbert York (who was Director of Research and Development in the Pentagon for many years and one of the President's scientific advisers) wrote of the 1972 treaty, SALT I, and the ABM treaty? He mentions the 'common understandings about basic issues' that were clearly implicit in that agreement between the United States . . .

NITZE: Which I think is quite wrong . . .

CHARLTON: . . . and the Soviet Union.

NITZE: There were no common understandings about that. We agreed on the language of several specific documents.

CHARLTON: So the idea that the ABM treaty reflected a common doctrine . . .

NITZE: . . . is nonsense.

CHARLTON: . . . among the two powers . . .

NITZE: . . . is nonsense. It's nonsense.

CHARLTON: . . . of 'mutual assured destruction' is not what you accept?

NITZE: It is nonsense, nonsense. The Russians were perfectly clear that they were not agreeing to anything beyond the specific obligations which they obligated themselves to abide by in the treaty and the associated documentation. There was a good deal of talk about this question as to whether one was agreeing to the 'spirit' of something that went beyond the pieces of paper – we *hoped* they would look at it that way. They did not.

CHARLTON: Well, one might have supposed, therefore, that you would have been less wholeheartedly committed yourself to the SALT I agreement if that doctrinal difference, which you've always drawn attention to and which is implicit in NSC 68, was still your view?

NITZE: No, it still was my view. But I still thought that the ABM treaty, specifically, could be – even though it had flaws in it, the most important of which was later cured in an agreement of 1978 – the ABM treaty could be made into a useful document. With respect to the Interim Agreement, Gerard Smith and I had recommended *against* the signing of the Interim Agreement which was part of SALT I. We thought that was too one-sidedly unfair to the United States. But when both pieces of paper were agreed concurrently, both Gerard Smith and I supported the package in the hope that, in the next two or three years, it would be possible to negotiate a new treaty, to parallel the ABM treaty, which would comprehensively and properly control offensive systems. But we were never able to get that.

NITZE'S MORE ABSOLUTE JUDGMENT contrasts with Henry Kissinger's search for common interest. Dr Kissinger's ambition had been to try to end the traditional American oscillation in foreign policy between, as he has said, 'extremes of intransigence and conciliation'. He had seen détente and arms control as a continuous process – an activity to be practised rather than a state that was reached. It was his complaint that SALT was unfairly made to bear the whole burden of East-West relations.

The advice given by the first representative to Imperial Russia of the London Muscovy Company in the days of Queen Elizabeth I was: 'When you deal with these people, make your bargains plain and put them in writing . . .' It became part of the critical assault mounted on the outcome of the arms control dialogue with the Russians that Kissinger's diplomatic virtuosity had taken too little account of this Elizabethan injunction. America had read into the record of the SALT I agreement some unilateral interpretations. This made such an agreement, as Eugene Rostow saw it, in certain vital respects little more than a promissory note.

EUGENE ROSTOW: There is a debate about what was permitted. You remember the controversy about 'unilateral interpretations' – there was a reason for those unilateral interpretations.
CHARLTON: You mean when the Secretary of State then, William Rogers, said he was giving a 'unilateral interpretation' to certain clauses which was clearly not, in terms of what happened in Vietnam and elsewhere, the interpretation given by the Soviet Union?
ROSTOW: Vietnam didn't have anything to do with it. The background to that affair was very different, and very interesting. It was the history of the Non-Proliferation Treaty. We took the position that under the treaty, if a 'European political entity' emerged, it would be considered a nuclear power by virtue of succession to the nuclear status of Britain and France. The Soviets said they could not agree publicly to any such statement, but if *we* made such a statement as an official interpretation of the Treaty, they would not publicly disagree with it, knowing the centrality of the independence of Western Europe to the American national interest. And that was done. Now what happened in 1972 was exactly the same, except with a different outcome. That is, the Soviets would not agree formally to unilateral interpretations – as I recall it, there were five of them. And the United States said, well then, we will announce these as 'unilateral interpretations' and expect you not to differ. They never differed in public, of course. They never said those are impermissible interpretations. What happened was, they went ahead and *built the weapons that President Nixon and Henry Kissinger thought were forbidden.*

CHARLTON: And which weapons were those?

ROSTOW: The SS-18s and SS-19s. There were several others, but the general build-up was of the big weapons, which we then recognised again in the SALT II treaty. It was a very, very devastating experience. We said we would abrogate the treaties – but then we didn't. The tangible advantages were that this changing nuclear balance permitted them to pursue with great energy a programme of expansion based on the use of conventional force. Vietnam was one example; the Middle East and the African adventures another. After all, the Cold War first began in Iran, with the Soviet probe toward Azerbaijan. It's now being conducted in the Caribbean, in the approaches to the Panama Canal. There's quite a difference.

THE FACT THAT THE GRANDCHILDREN of Lenin stand today on the southern doorstep of the United States makes the obvious point that the East-West conflict spares no part of the world. The central thrust of the argument made by the Committee on the Present Danger was that the change in the nuclear balance was radiating new perceptions of opportunity and anxiety. The American confidence with which President Kennedy had acted against Khruschev's diplomacy by intimidation in the Caribbean was to be contrasted with American hesitation as a new generation of revolutionaries and guerrillas supported by Moscow pulled Central America into the mainstream of world history. The loss of the strategic superiority President Kennedy had enjoyed could prevent the United States from using its conventional forces to defend its interests (as Kennedy had threatened to do).

Arms control negotiations had failed to eliminate this coercive circumstance. The powerful opposition of Senator Henry Jackson in the Congress had all but nullified Kissinger's détente policy. When allied with the crusade of the Committee on the Present Danger, it formed a hyphen of bipartisan support to President Reagan's later call for the militarisation of foreign policy. Whereas Kissinger had considered that America could not keep its alliances together without dedication to arms control, this new consensus was overtly sceptical.

Senator Jackson's former associate Richard Perle, who drafted much of the Senator's unyielding opposition to SALT, is now President Reagan's Assistant Secretary for Defence. Should it be acknowledged, therefore, that by that time the Soviet Union possessed a *superior* insight into the military and political utility of nuclear weapons – and the function of arms control?

RICHARD PERLE: A different insight, and an insight that I think was based in part on Soviet judgments about the West, about the willingness of the West to match the Soviet Union. But I think one should also say that if there *was* a superior insight on the part of the Soviet Union, it was into the nature of the arms control process, and how arms control might be used to facilitate a continuing Soviet build-up with greatly diminished apprehension in the West. I can't think of a comparable period in world history in which one of two adversary states was permitted to expand its military forces on the scale of the Soviet expansion (between, say, 1970 and 1980) without arousing the most profound apprehensions in the other adversary state. I think the unrealised hopes for arms control (and the attendant psychology), and the political détente that we sought, had the effect of permitting that build-up to take place without producing the normal reactions one would have expected at any other time in world history. I think the history of arms control is not terribly encouraging, and I find the passion for it out of all proportion to its historical record.

CHARLTON: Can arms control play any meaningful role in meeting the strategic requirements of the United States?

PERLE: That remains to be seen. In theory one can construct agreements that are fair to both sides, and diminish the threat faced by both sides – and produce a higher degree of stability. But we won't know whether such agreements can be signed until we put them on the table and demonstrate the *patience* to test fully the Soviet willingness to join in such agreements. If we repeat the mistake of the past, which is to table proposals of roughly that nature, only to fall back in the give and take of negotiation – ultimately, to sign agreements that do *not* meet that test – then I think the Soviets much prefer doing business that way and that is the way we will continue to do business.

CHARLTON: Would you agree that the West Europeans place arms control and the superpower dialogue ahead of, higher in importance than issues about the nuclear balance? How do you see the significance of that?

PERLE: I think it's very foolish indeed. Not only because there is no historical justification for the confidence in arms control that one would expect, given the enthusiasm for it from the Europeans. But all the arms control agreements in the world are not going to protect our security or our interests if the military balance is permitted to deteriorate; if it becomes adverse to the West to the point where the Soviet Union feels it can exert pressure; and if the West in turn feels it cannot resist. There is no reason why we should abandon arms control. It is important to remain realistic about its prospects and tenacious in negotiating. I think that if it fails to produce results, so long as we have made reasonable proposals, proposals that we can defend (the Soviets don't have to defend their proposals in quite the same way, certainly not to their own people) – then I think we can sustain even quite a long period *without* agreement, as long as we are seen to be attempting to obtain a *good* agreement.

RICHARD PERLE REJECTS THE VIEW that in arms control the process itself is almost as important as the result. By the late 1970s, what proved to be the ascendant branch of thinking among American policy makers considered that the effort to persuade the Soviet Union to accept strategic concepts which Marxist-Leninist ideology rejected had demonstrably failed. This analysis of a Soviet Union prepared to fight and to win a nuclear war was sustained by its perceived ability to do so. Unlike the United States (which had rejected the proposition in Kennedy's time), they had a civil defence programme to diminish their casualties; and the Soviet Union's achievement of superiority in land-based offensive missiles threatened the opportunity of a first strike against the American land-based force. That threat, in turn, made American nuclear strength no longer a deterrent against Soviet expansion. But for the statesman, faced with destiny's challenge in this dialogue with the Russians over nuclear arms, was it – *is* it – inevitable that relations had to be governed by the inveterate pessimism of 'the worst possible case'?

PAUL NITZE: Is 'the worst possible case' always worse than what happens? Who suspected Pearl Harbour would occur? Who suspected that Hitler would really be as dreadful as he turned out to be? You know, the worst possible case is generally worse than the imagination can imagine. But what you have to deal with really is what are the logical and most probable cases. You can't deal with the 'worst possible' cases.

CHARLTON: But I ask you that as a diplomat rather than, let us say, a Chairman of the Joint Chiefs of Staff who is charged with a narrower, or rather different, responsibility. As a *diplomat*, do you still feel that in these circumstances, presented with a phenomenon like this, there is no alternative other than to accept the pessimistic scenario?

NITZE: No, I don't believe it to be pessimistic! That's what I'm quarrelling with you about. I believe there is no point in looking at the world other than with open eyes, and accepting facts as they are. Why should one ignore facts? That road is sure to lead to disaster.

CHARLTON: It's very important, I think, that we should understand the issue you made of the Soviet advantage (or perceived advantage) in their big land-based missile. You spoke and wrote at the time that the Soviet Union 'was pursuing a theoretical war-winning capability'. Does that mean that you accept that the edge they had with this big missile did not represent a real disarming first-strike capability?

NITZE: Yes. What I had in mind was that it represented a real first-strike disarming capability against fixed land-based targets in the United States and in the rest of NATO. But it did not represent an ability to take out at least a portion of our bomber force, that portion which was on alert and ready to take off at a few minutes' notice: and it did not include those sea-launched ballistic missiles at sea. So it did not have a *true* disarming capability, because what was left would still be able to deny the Soviet Union any real advantages, any *political* advantages, from a military attack.

It would still leave the Soviet Union with great *military* advantages. It would leave them in a position where they could undoubtedly aspire to win, in military terms, a nuclear war – in other words, to be in a position where they could end that war favourably to themselves. It would not be one from which any sensible Soviet would wish to *initiate* because of the vast damage which would be done to the Soviet Union.

So I have never said that we lost the capability of deterrence. I think we still have a good deterrent; but, I repeat, I think the Soviets have an advantage in those forces which count with respect to ending up or being in a superior military position during a war. And you know, there is only one thing worse than having a nuclear war, and that's to lose a nuclear war.

CHARLTON: What were the political advantages, as you see them, which possession of this large missile conferred upon the Russians in the practical conduct of policy? Are there things you would point to?

NITZE: Yes. For instance, during the Cuban missile crisis. You know, no one could be certain that one could weave through that Cuban missile crisis without a danger of some kind of military confrontation with the Soviet Union. We had complete tactical advantage – that is, non-nuclear advantage – in the area of Cuba. We also had, I thought, a very substantial strategic nuclear advantage at the time of the Cuban missile crisis. But even then, we were not quite certain that it couldn't run into some risk that war would occur – or nuclear weapons be used. The chances were one in a hundred or a thousand or something like that. But *today*, you know, those risks would be greater. Today we would operate in such a situation with much less confidence than we did then. That gives the Soviets a considerable advantage. You see what they're doing in Africa, in the Middle East, what they're doing in Afghanistan – today, there is literally no possibility that the West could possibly consider doing anything about it. And that has also been true in Poland and other places. I think the *security* the Soviets have had in going forward with these various things around the world, bit by bit, means they haven't been concerned about any military opposition by the West to those things – *because they have such clear military superiority*. And, of course, they get advantages from that in addition to prestige.

CHARLTON: And if one takes the Cuban crisis, your reading is that the nuclear equation – America's strategic nuclear superiority – determined the outcome in the end?

NITZE: No, I didn't say that. I find *others* have said that it had no bearing – because we had conventional superiority. We had both. It's very hard when you have both to say which one is the determining one. It's the combination of both which was relevant there.

CHARLTON: So those who deny that the nuclear component had any influence over the outcome . . .

NITZE: I think they're clearly wrong. It had some. All I'm trying to say is that we had both conventional *and* nuclear superiority, and we *still* thought the risks were not minimal. I know the President thought the risks were really quite great. But he was still determined to go forward with it.

CHARLTON: As a man who has sat across the table from the Russians in endless hours of negotiation and argument about these nuclear issues over the years, what in that experience reinforces your conviction that they *set out* to achieve, in their strategic weapons forces, that superiority which you maintain is there?

NITZE: Well, at one time during SALT I, I talked to my opposite number, a very distinguished Soviet scientist, about a way in which we could really achieve a set of systems between the two sides which would give complete deterrence to both sides; which would assure the Soviet Union that there would be no possibility that the United States could attack them (with any possibility of gaining thereby), and there would be no possibility that the Soviet Union could attack *us* with any possibility of gaining thereby. This was to eliminate all our existing ICBMs and substitute a far larger number, say even 5000, *small* ICBMs – each one of which was so small that it could not be 'MIRVed'. So then you would have 5000 on both sides that could not be 'MIRVed'. Anybody who attacked the other (because you could not get perfect reliability) would be sure to lose more of his weapons than he would take out of the other side's weapons; and this number was sufficiently large that it would protect against cheating, or third countries, and so forth. This, I said, would really work. And my Soviet opposite number said, 'I couldn't agree with you more. It would in fact do exactly what you say it would do. But we're not going to do it. We like our big weapons. Our military in particular like our big weapons. We've put a lot of effort into those big weapons and we're just not going to give them up.'

CHARLTON: How do you counter those who say that the failure to ratify the SALT II agreement meant that the advantage they have is augmented: that they can build up to a level far beyond your own present capabilities in warheads *without* SALT II, but *with* it they would have been more restricted and confined?

NITZE: Both sides have lived up to both SALT I and SALT II during the entire period since 1971 when SALT was ratified. And look at what's happened in that period. During that period, the Soviets have increased the number of their warheads by a factor of four. They have increased what is called their 'prompt hard-target kill' capability by a factor of ten. That is all *within* the terms of SALT I and SALT II. So it would seem perfectly clear that SALT I and SALT II were not going to do anything to restrain the Soviet Union, or really to restrain us. We have not been restrained in the West from doing anything we really wanted to do by either SALT I or SALT II over this entire period. So it was a 'nothing agreement'.

I never did say to the Senate that they should *not* ratify. I said you can make up your mind whether you want to ratify – that's your task. But you really ought to understand it. You ought to understand that *it limits the wrong things*. Its purported limits on new types are really very confusing, and it is dubious whether they will turn out the way we expect them to turn out. It has all kinds of defects. Now, if you really want to ratify it *after* understanding its defects, that's up to you!

EMANATING AS IT DID from a 'Captain at the Gate' like Paul Nitze, of long experience and respected opinion in defence matters, such 'multi-conditional' assent to SALT II had wide influence, proving to be a new bipartisan bridge to President Reagan's policies – it arched over the Carter Administration and the closing years of the 1970s, with their increasing strain and stalemate over the conduct of arms control and détente. By Nitze's measurement, the application of arms control agreements had furthered neither restraint nor stability based upon the central 'balance of terror'. While diplomats persisted in their search, technical advances and ideological imperatives were constantly making stability elusive. The optimists had been rejoicing in 'mutual assured destruction', complacent or unheeding that the deterrent threat of nuclear weapons was becoming less and less plausible.

Four years ago, in 1982, Richard Nixon (who had ordered a nuclear alert at the time of the Yom Kippur war in the Middle East in 1973) argued that, even if America restores the balance in nuclear forces, 'We will not fully restore their deterrent effect, as in crises like the Cuban missile crisis and the Arab-Israeli War in 1973. A threat of mutual suicide is simply not credible.' Henry Kissinger considered that it was 'sheer escapism' to yearn for a past that technology now proscribed; overwhelming superiority could not be recaptured. But containment, which was not just the slogan but the inspiration of bipartisanship in American foreign policy, rested on superiority. Therefore, wasn't the corollary of nuclear parity the probability that there would be increased *instability* at the lower levels of rivalry and conflict?

EUGENE ROSTOW: No, not a bit. The implicit premise – and I think this is the essence of the entire problem – of what Truman said, and what Kennedy said, and what Eisenhower said, and all the spokesmen of American policy and Western policy generally throughout the early period said, was that the Western nations were going to oppose aggression against their interests. That is what Korea means, when you have Ethiopian troops going to Korea and Turkish troops going to Korea. Ethiopian troops especially were a symbol of a policy which said we made a profound mistake in the 1930s in not stopping Mussolini in Ethiopia – and we are not going to make that mistake again. This time we are going to prevent a general war by stopping small wars. It was the reaction to that experience in Korea, then most emphatically in Vietnam afterwards, that led the West to scratch its head and say there must be a better way of reaching agreement than that. Because the Soviets did not stop, you see. They kept right on coming.

CHARLTON: Isn't that an important distinction in your own view of what deterrence should be? Deterrence to you is not the status quo, stability in that sense. There is an element of compulsion about it, of coercion; that is, getting the Soviet Union, or aiming to get the Soviet Union, to do something which it is not at present doing.

ROSTOW: That's correct. What we're trying to persuade them to do through deterrence – through collective security – is to respect the rules of the United Nations Charter against aggression. It is the only code we have representing at least a nominal agreement among the powers as to the rules of behaviour in international affairs. Those rules are not an invention or a dream. They go back to the Congress of Vienna, and to the whole experience of the state system. Now what's happened is, when you talk to a Soviet diplomat or for that matter a Soviet professor of law about that, he says: 'You're asking us to give up a foreign policy rooted in our nature as a society and in the state.' In other words, they're saying, 'We have a right as leader of the Socialist Commonwealth to use force for aggressive purposes against states, and you don't.' Well, that is an untenable position; and unless it's changed, it's bound to lead to the most ghastly explosion.

CHARLTON: But how can it be changed? How can the Soviet Union be *deterred* from its world view, its 'historic mission'?

ROSTOW: There are only one or two ways in which that can be done, given the folly of American policy during the 1970s in failing to keep pace with the Soviet drive for nuclear superiority. We can build like mad, which is a very disagreeable thought – Midgetmen and Minutemen and MXs and so on. We can develop the defensive weapons, which of course is what's happening now. The Soviets have put an enormous effort into that and President Reagan really had no choice but to match it. It's very much like the choice presented to Roosevelt about the first nuclear weapon, when the scientists came to him and said, 'Hitler is making nuclear arms'. President Roosevelt did not have a choice. He *had* to go ahead.

EUGENE ROSTOW, who has served four Presidents from Roosevelt to Reagan, has carried us forward to the political origins of the 'Star Wars' proposal, and the answer it might give to Henry Kissinger's question as he contemplated the baroque superfluity of destructive power in the nuclear arsenals of America and Russia: 'What in the name of God is strategic superiority? What do you do with it?'

The view of the Soviet Union held by Paul Nitze and his associates, which had guided the American policy of containment during the Cold War, gained the high ground once more in the failure of Jimmy Carter's Presidency and in the more confident use of military force by the Russians. Henry Kissinger's détente faltered in the sands of Ethiopia, and it was finally buried among the harsh hills of Afghanistan in the wake of another Soviet invasion. In the Carter years, Republicans and Democrats of the American foreign policy establishment, who had upheld the bipartisan policies of deterrence and containment ever since World War II, were divided on almost every topic. Americans found no clear political will.

4

MUTUAL ASSURED DESTRUCTION:

President Carter Sounds Retreat

THE FOUR YEARS OF Jimmy Carter's Presidency, from 1976 to 1980, ended in the total eclipse of détente with the Soviet Union. Events in those four years galvanised the American strategic debate, and they included Presidential Directive 59 – a new shadow on the cave wall of nuclear deterrence. In his famous treatise about an ideal political saviour, Machiavelli considered that the concept of necessity must govern the actions of the statesman. He can only decide what is necessary if the statesman has a clear picture of the realities of the world in which he must act, including the ethical compromises he must tolerate. By this measurement, and in the end by his own admission, Jimmy Carter's Presidency had failed. Carter began his Administration by saying that American strategic policy had been based on an outdated view of the world – the belief that Soviet expansion must be contained. As his Administration was ending, he announced that the Russian invasion of Afghanistan had caused him to revise drastically his appraisal of Soviet intentions.

Jimmy Carter had offered to restore the American sense of moral righteousness in the lurid afterglow of President Nixon's impeachment and the loss of the Vietnam War. America turned to him with a sentimental appreciation. Individual human rights – the antithesis of Communism, which deems such rights to be collective only – were installed by Carter as almost a new commandment and identified as the most compelling force for political change. 'Being confident of our own future', said President Carter in 1977, 'we are now free of that inordinate fear of Communism which once led us to embrace any dictator who joined us in that fear.' In practice this meant that strategically important allies of the United States were at times denounced for their violations of human rights. The writing was on the wall for the Shah of Persia and for the 'Nixon doctrine' which – in the aftermath of Britain's withdrawal from her historical responsibilities in the Persian Gulf – had made Iran a pillar of American security in the area.

Jimmy Carter did not, in the end, succeed in overcoming these inherent contradictions in strategic policy. The new President came to office an enthusiast for arms control and believed it to be the principal activity in the Soviet-American relationship. He brought to the issue deep-seated personal convictions about the moral and strategic implications of 'the arms race'. President Carter had a more ambitious and immediate objective for the SALT process, and it bore the influence of critics of Henry Kissinger's détente such as Senator 'Scoop' Jackson, but he opened with an ambiguity – two proposals.

PRESIDENT CARTER: When I first decided to run for President, one of the most important issues that I had to study was the history of arms control negotiations with the Soviet Union – the techniques of negotiation (on both sides), the overall goals of the Soviets and of my own predecessors, the scope of the agreements reached, the commitment by us and the Soviets to comply with the agreements – and the remaining work to be done. I was impressed by the fact that all my predecessors had been successful – beginning with John Kennedy, through Johnson, Nixon and Ford, in concluding agreements with the Soviet Union. I wanted to go much further than they had gone, but I saw the great advantage of proceeding in an evolutionary fashion: that is, building upon the foundation that they had laid before me. The single challenge that I had, that was the most important, was to conclude the SALT II treaty which, in all, had required about six-and-a-half years under three Presidents.

CHARLTON: To what extent were your own intentions based on differing assumptions from those which had guided Nixon and Kissinger?

PRESIDENT CARTER: I wanted to have a much more dramatic reduction in nuclear arsenals. I wanted to build to it what I considered to be a penultimate arrangement, that is, a small number of *single*-warhead missiles (with the missiles all uniform in size), and deploy them in a totally invulnerable place. This was my goal. So, within two months after I had taken office, I sent Secretary Vance to Moscow with the first step toward the realisation of this goal. He had a dual proposal to put forward. One was just a cautious evolutionary building upon the Vladivostok agreement.[1] The other was a much sharper reduction – which the Soviets rejected out of hand and seemed to take as insincere, which was regrettable.

CHARLTON: What do you remember as being the controlling idea in your mind about taking all the negotiating risks you did, in departing from previous practice and seeking really dramatic *cuts* in the nuclear arsenals of both sides?

[1] negotiated by Henry Kissinger in the Ford Administration

PRESIDENT CARTER: I really didn't put too much emphasis on the risks involved, you know. I knew what I wanted to do. I saw myself concluding a SALT II treaty (which would have to be an interim agreement) and then moving immediately to a SALT III agreement, which would be much more drastic in its cuts, and which would also include intermediate-range missiles in the overall reductions. So this was the departure from what Presidents Nixon and Ford, and others, had done. They had had very limited agreements. In fact, the *words* they used were 'limited agreements', with 'threshold bans' and so forth. I wanted to have a comprehensive test ban – to eliminate completely the testing of all nuclear explosives. I also wanted to eliminate, totally, any use of space for the deployment of *defensive* or *offensive* weaponry.

I had three simultaneous negotiations under way. One was with the Pentagon, the Joint Chiefs of Staff and the Secretary of Defence and his associates. The second one was with the key members of the Congress, particularly in the Senate. The third, of course, was with the Soviets. I had to do them all in 'lock-step'; I couldn't get too far ahead with any one before I proceeded with the others. We never put forward a negotiating position, either in the Cabinet Room with Dobrynin[2] or Gromyko[3] or at Vienna with President Brezhnev, which had not been previously cleared and supported by the Joint Chiefs, Secretary of Defence Harold Brown, and also his associates in the Pentagon.

I recognised that members of the Senate would be a much more difficult challenge because a substantial number of the senators will never support any agreement with the Soviet Union; nor one that involves the United Nations, nor one that puts any constraints on our own ability to build our military arsenals. That was the most difficult. At the same time, the Soviets are tough negotiators. I knew this to be a fact before I was inaugurated as President. They had their own particular plans to protect – as we did.

My impression then was that the Soviets were, indeed, observing the agreements previously reached. That fact was confirmed to me by Secretary Kissinger when he came down here, to Plains[4], to brief me even before I was sworn in as President. And so I had a sense, first of all, that the Soviets negotiated in good faith; secondly, that they *did* carry out the terms of an agreement once reached (with some small violations on both sides), and thirdly, that my restraints were just as much with the Senate as they were at the bargaining table with the Soviets.

CHARLTON: But in the back of your mind, was there a conviction that there were rational men in Moscow who had to share your intentions and assumptions?

PRESIDENT CARTER: Yes . . . I would not say 'conviction'. There was certainly a hope and an expectation. I had to realise that the Soviets were

[2] Anatoly Dobrynin, Soviet Ambassador to the US
[3] Andrei Gromyko, then Soviet Foreign Minister
[4] President Carter's home in Plains, Georgia

not trustful of us and our intentions. They see the actions taken by the Senate. They heard the aftermath of the SALT I treaty, when the President was condemned for 'selling out' the American interest. They are heavily influenced by statements out of Washington of a belligerent nature.

I recognised, too, that the Soviets could only go so far in their reductions, on an *equal basis* with the United States, before the arsenals of Great Britain, France and China became a factor. So I saw the restraints and limitations on what I could do. But I was insistent always, I think, until the day I went out of office to *cut* as much as the Soviets would possibly accept, and not be timid about the political consequences.

CHARLTON: You took that decision in the face of advice, it would seem, from your Secretary of State, Cyrus Vance, who has written since that he disagreed with it. He said he thought the President's decision to 'jump over SALT II', as I think he put it, 'was a long shot'. May I ask again, was there one controlling idea for you in your determination to come to grips with the technological and doctrinal impulses of the 'arms race' in a quite new way?

PRESIDENT CARTER: I think the 'controlling' idea was one that I expressed in my speech at Georgia Tech: that is, progress on arms control was a good way to ease the tensions that had built up between our country and the Soviets in many other (and non-related) issues. An absence of arms control was likely to exacerbate regional conflicts or the regional competition that existed. And so I saw this as not only a way to reduce actual levels of nuclear armaments, but also to lay a diplomatic base for progress in dealing with the Soviets on a dual track. One was co-operation, wherever possible; the other was competition, on a peaceful basis whenever necessary.

CHARLTON: Vance says that although he'd advised you not to go ahead with the 'deep cuts' proposal, he was nonetheless angered in Moscow by 'the finality and the vehemence' (as he put it) with which Brezhnev rejected your SALT proposals. What were your own reactions?

PRESIDENT CARTER: I don't recall Vance's advising against it, but I wouldn't dispute what he said. *I* was disappointed and angered by the vehemence of the Soviet rejection. Gromyko called an unprecedented press conference after they were given our proposals, and talked as much about our human rights policy as he did about nuclear arms control. But, at the same time, we didn't send an *ultimatum* to the Soviet Union – we didn't send just one proposal, we sent them the dual proposal. One was the very gradual step, building upon the Vladivostok agreement; and the other one a much more dramatic step with 'deep cuts', to let them have their choice.

CHARLTON: But surprised, or angered, as you were by the vehemence with which Brezhnev rejected your proposals for big reductions in strategic weapons (which, after all, had been publicly articulated Soviet policy for many years), what construction were you inclined to place on it as you worked further into your administration?

PRESIDENT CARTER: I felt the reason was probably two-fold. One was aversion to our human rights policy. Brezhnev looked upon this as a gratuitous attack on his country, on his system of government, on Soviet society under Communist rule – which was not the case. Our human rights policy was universal in application and applied as much to other countries, even to ourselves, as it did to the Soviet Union. The other one was, I think, the Soviets operate by consensus . . .

CHARLTON: In the Politburo you mean?

PRESIDENT CARTER: . . . in the Politburo, and there's also a large committee of about three hundred people who vet these things quite thoroughly in a debate. Then the Politburo members, a smaller group of around a dozen leaders, make a decision. The President of the Soviet Union, or the General-Secretary now, is just the spokesman for a board of directors. It's impossible for them to act in a peremptory way, or in anything other than a very slow, evolutionary process.

I think that they were disturbed by the fact that I wanted to move much more aggressively than they did. I think they doubted our intentions. Whether they were propagandising, or whether they thought that we were acting in an insincere fashion, or whether Brezhnev thought that we were rejecting the Vladivostok progress, or whether they were just showing their anger over our human rights policy, I've never been able to discern. I think only the Soviets who were in the Politburo meeting could make that analysis.

PRESIDENT CARTER ECHOES that persistent and corrosive theme in the Soviet-American relationship – the doubt and mistrust engendered by the isolation and secrecy in which the Soviet party-governmental apparatus functions and reaches its decisions. It remains an aspect in which (Henry Kissinger's diplomatic virtuosity notwithstanding) not much seems to have changed since Basil Liddell-Hart, the British military historian, remarked that even when they were partners in the war against Hitler, the western Allies were 'much more in the dark about the Soviet forces and intentions than about the German . . .'.

The initial attitude of the Carter Presidency to SALT reflected a different view, and was less certain of the political (and military) usefulness of nuclear weapons, than its predecessors. Carter's men questioned publicly whether the Soviet Union could derive political advantages from its more powerful force of land-based missiles and their perceived ability to threaten the American land-based Minutemen with a first strike. As we've previously heard, such political advantage from the changing nuclear balance was believed by some leading Democrats (including Paul Nitze, Gene Rostow and their associates who formed the Committee on the Present Danger) to be the very embodiment of Soviet intentions. That ex-nuclear submariner, President Carter, was more sanguine.

PRESIDENT CARTER: Some people have a morbid fear of Soviet capabilities
– I've never shared that fear. I think that in a peaceful competition we have
all the advantages on our side. I've never been convinced at all that the
Soviets had a superiority in the military field. I think we still have an overall
military superiority, and this would certainly include the nuclear arsenals
on both sides.

The Soviets have a psychological need to be looked upon as equals. They
are driven by this, in my opinion, to prove to the world that they are an
equal to the other superpower. We've never felt this urge to have to *prove*
that we were one of the superpowers, or that we were indeed equal. I think
we have a natural feeling that we are, in many ways, superior to the Soviet
Union. That superior-inferior relationship is something that the Soviets
constantly strive to overcome.

There has never been a time when the Soviets have effectively used the
threat of nuclear weaponry to achieve their regional goals. The only times
we have seen nuclear arsenals put on 'stand-by alert' on a worldwide basis
have been outgrowths of the Middle East conflict – and I think that's a
most likely place for potential explosion in the future that would involve
superpower confrontations.

CHARLTON: But if the nuclear dimension played a role in determining the
outcome over Cuba for Kennedy, would a similar situation have the same
outcome today?

PRESIDENT CARTER: No. I think that we couldn't effectively force the
Soviets to yield now by the threat of using nuclear weaponry, as Kennedy
was able to do.

CHARLTON: Doesn't that, with great respect, contradict what you've just
said? That is how they *do*, in fact, manipulate crises?

PRESIDENT CARTER: No. I think the Soviets have built their nuclear
arsenals up to a rough equivalency, so they are no longer forced to yield.
But they have not built them up to a level of superiority where they can
hope to make *us* yield. So I think there is a stand-off in nuclear weaponry.

THIS STAND-OFF WAS DUE in part to a considerable change in the
President's original attitude to the state of the nuclear balance. He had
been at first dismissive of the threat of a Soviet first strike, and the
multiplication of Soviet missiles and nuclear warheads. In his inaugural
address in January 1977, Jimmy Carter said, 'We will move this year a step
toward our ultimate goal – the elimination of all nuclear weapons from
this earth. . . .' And Carter had indeed begun by cancelling or delaying the
introduction of new weapons, such as the B–1 bomber, the so-called
Neutron Bomb, Trident and MX. But within two years – the Russians
having rejected his proposal for dramatic reductions in the nuclear
arsenals – Jimmy Carter was faced with the decision to deploy two
additional missiles, Trident II and MX, to compensate for what was now
more widely seen as a growing American disadvantage.

In the first chapter, Robert McNamara (President Kennedy's and President Johnson's Defence Secretary) maintained his conviction that 'a cycle of action and reaction' was the dynamic fuel of the arms race. The passing of another fifteen years of nuclear experience had brought one of McNamara's successors to an opposite conclusion. Some utterances have hung in the air above the protracted struggle of the nuclear debate, among them Kissinger's ironical question about strategic superiority. Another had resonance in and beyond the Carter Presidency – those uncomfortable words spoken by Dr Harold Brown, President Carter's Defence Secretary.

HAROLD BROWN: 'When we build, they build – and when we don't build, they build.' Yes, I guess that will be carved on my tombstone, and I still believe it is correct. What that was meant to convey was that Soviet defence programmes – and this is not by any means confined to strategic programmes and, in the context of my remark, it clearly was not limited to strategic programmes – go on the basis of an *internal* logic, and the much-quoted 'action-reaction cycles' had only very modest reality. The Soviets have their own programmes, they have their own objectives; and although we can limit them by arms control agreements, we are not likely to know exactly why they're willing to accept some limits.

CHARLTON: What deductions follow in terms of your testimony that when we build, they build – and when we do not, they go on building? What deductions are valid in terms of American policy?

BROWN: There are two deductions that, I think, follow from that. One is that the United States needs to decide what its requirements are for strategic or conventional forces, in terms of what we now see as the threats. We can project the threats for three or four years 'down the road' pretty well, simply because we know that's how long it takes to turn decisions into test programmes, or test programmes into deployments. So we need to decide that for ourselves. The second thing, oddly enough, is that there is one way to influence Soviet military programmes, and that's by arms control. We can influence by arms control agreements far better than we can influence them by our example or by our doctrinal writings – because they may not follow our example, and they may not share our doctrines.

CHARLTON: Can I just remind you of something you said, as Defence Secretary, in a speech to the US Naval Academy, where you pointed out that the Soviets had been embarked for more than a decade on a policy of building forces for a pre-emptive strike on US intercontinental missiles? By the early 1980s, you said, the Soviet Union would possess sufficient numbers of the new big missile, the SS–18, to assure the destruction of the vast majority of Minutemen in a surgically precise and surprise attack. Doesn't that come very close to the critique made by the Committee on the Present Danger? That these kinds of agreements were fundamentally flawed because they had admitted this kind of activity — and the United States had agreed to it?

BROWN: The United States, in its SALT agreements, never sought a guarantee that some individual element of its forces would be safe from pre-emptive attack by the Soviet Union independent of what the United States did. It is true that the Soviet build-up, aimed at giving them this capability for pre-emptive attack on one element of the US retaliatory force, had by dint of what they had done during the 1970s succeeded. This then was a *fact*, whether or not the Soviet Union had an intention of launching a pre-emptive attack in the face of certain retaliation from the bombers and the submarine-launched ballistic missiles.

At the time I made that speech, the United States had a programme that would have deployed new missiles in multiple protective shelters and in numbers that would have prevented the Soviet Union from being able to attack even *that* element of the US retaliatory force successfully. So when I made that speech there was, in place, a US programme to remove this element of vulnerability, and a SALT II agreement whose ratification would have assured a limitation on the number of Soviet warheads. So I posed a threat, and I said what we were doing to respond to it. Both elements of that response were cast aside during the subsequent year. The result is that US forces which would have included a relatively invulnerable land-based component by the mid-1980s will now not include such a component, at least into the 1990s.

THEY WERE 'CAST ASIDE' in the Reagan Administration, not least because new events had overgrown the whole context of SALT. In consequence, the SALT II agreement, signed by Carter and Brezhnev in Vienna in 1979, was never ratified in Washington — although both sides still adhere to the limits of missiles then agreed.

In a treaty by which the enemies or antagonists promise to limit their nuclear arsenals, the central problem is 'stability through equality'. Henry Kissinger records in his memoirs that Brezhnev could not solicit often enough Kissinger's avowal that America would proceed in its dealings with the Soviet Union on the premise of equality. In the Carter years both pillars of the proposition, stability and equality, were being sharply questioned within the American strategic debate, as it weighed in the balance the huge Soviet rearmament programme being carried out during the period of détente. How, then, did President Carter judge for himself the scale and intentions of Soviet armament, and of what his Defence Secretary Harold Brown had said: 'When we build, they build — and when we don't build, they build'?

PRESIDENT CARTER: One interpretation to be placed on it is that the Soviets were so far behind in nuclear weaponry, and they were deeply embarrassed by the Cuban missile crisis when they were branded as inferior to us in nuclear capability.

CHARLTON: As Kuznetsov (the Deputy Foreign Minister) said at the time: 'You will never get away with this again!'

PRESIDENT CARTER: He said, 'It will never happen again.' So I think they proceeded aggressively to make sure that they were at least equal to us.

CHARLTON: Is that the explanation you favour yourself?

PRESIDENT CARTER: I think the Soviets are inclined to be paranoid. We look upon the Soviets as trying to equal or exceed US armament capabilities. We are almost always ahead of them in technological advances: miniaturisation of circuits; the dependability of solid-fuel rockets; guidance systems; accuracy; the 'MIRVing' of missiles. We've always been ahead of them, almost always, in these areas. And we've always thought that our advantages would last five to ten years – and they've generally lasted from one to two years. The Soviets are quite quick in catching up.

The things that the Soviets had at the beginning because of necessity later turned out to be an advantage. For instance, they had missiles (the SS–18s, SS–19s) that they had to build because they did not know how to miniaturise circuitry. Once 'MIRVing' came along at our initiative, the Soviets had these enormous missiles to carry very large multiple-warhead payloads. That's another factor.

I think another one that we tend to overlook – I'm trying to put myself in the Soviet position – is that they don't see themselves facing just the United States. They also see as potential adversaries China – of whom they have a morbid fear for some reason – and also Great Britain and France, whom they look upon as NATO allies of ours. So they add all those arsenals together, the four arsenals, and try to equal them . . .

CHARLTON: Or wish to have a superiority over all?

PRESIDENT CARTER: That's right, and I'm not sure that our country has ever been willing, or ever will be willing, to accept genuine equality. What we define as equality almost inevitably is going to be superiority. I think we do at this time have superiority.

CHARLTON: Interesting that you mention this word 'equality' – which is fundamental, isn't it? Is it in your view desirable, or achievable, with the Soviet Union?

PRESIDENT CARTER: It's desirable. But I don't think it is achievable because the measurements are so highly distorted by the different perspectives from the two nations. We look upon their very large missiles as being a threat which we will never match. The Soviets look upon our Cruise missiles, our 'stealth' capabilities being evolved; the relative invulnerability of our missile submarines with their extreme quietness; our advanced anti-submarine warfare; the Soviets' constraints on their submarines entering the major oceans and our easy access to warm oceans almost immediately from our harbours – they look upon these advantages of ours with a great deal of concern.

ALTHOUGH CONCERNED, THE RUSSIANS seemed less inhibited by the sense of risk. Eighteen months into Jimmy Carter's Presidency, they made a dynamic new thrust which placed fresh strains on US–Soviet relations. A Soviet airlift of Cuban forces into Ethiopia in 1977 assumed the pattern of the similar airlift into Angola two years before, immediately following that time in America when, in the words of Henry Kissinger, 'we destroyed a President'. This time, the Soviet presence in Ethiopia came to be viewed as a challenge in a strategically important part of the world, the Horn of Africa, and a threat to the SALT negotiations. President Carter determined to safeguard the priority of a second SALT treaty when he said: 'I will not let the pressure of inevitable competition with the Soviet Union overwhelm possibilities for co-operation.'

But the Soviet intervention raised the old and undismissable issue of 'linkage'. Kissinger had said that the Soviet Union could not have the 'atmosphere' of détente without the substance. The presumption underlying US arms control policy and détente policies had been a reciprocal Soviet restraint. The issue of 'linkage' divided the Carter Cabinet, and the President did not resolve that division. The National Security Adviser, Zbigniew Brzezinski, said that for him 'détente was buried in the sands of the Ogaden in Ethiopia'. And the President?

PRESIDENT CARTER: I never felt that way. Brzezinski was much more inclined to want to link the arms control efforts with the inevitable competition between us and the Soviets on extending influence. One of my major goals was to decrease the Soviet influence in the Middle East by carrying out an agreement that would extend *our own* influence and lessen that of the Soviets. Another goal I had was in the western part of the Pacific. I did not normalise relations with China just to minimise Soviet influence, but that obviously was one of the results of it. So I think that this inclination of Dr Brzezinski to tie the two together was not compatible with my own. I basically agreed with Harold Brown and Secretary Vance, who felt just the other way.
CHARLTON: But – exactly. It clearly was a very great difficulty for you, was it not, throughout your Administration? You were riding two horses, really, in terms of policy, and with increasing difficulty.
PRESIDENT CARTER: Well, everybody has to ride two horses on policy as it relates to the Soviet Union. You can't put your total investment in confrontation and belligerence toward the Soviet Union. This might be politically popular, but it's counter-productive for our nation. The best approach, I think, to the Soviets is what I have described in very simplistic terms. That is, co-operate whenever you can (with trade agreements, with SALT agreements and so forth), and compete with them when you have to – which suited me fine.
CHARLTON: Cyrus Vance, in what he wrote after the end of the Carter Administration, mentions acerbic exchanges that you had with Gromyko

over this Horn of Africa intervention by the Soviet Union and Cuba, and the feeling that you had been deceived by Gromyko. What took place between you?

PRESIDENT CARTER: Well, we have the technical capability to monitor radio broadcasts – particularly along the sea coast, like Ethiopia and the Ogaden. We were quite familiar with which Soviet military leaders were in Ethiopia. We knew when one of them was ill, or when one had to go back to the Soviet Union to attend his son's wedding, or when a replacement was ordered to Ethiopia. Gromyko came to the Cabinet Room and was giving the Politburo line (which I presume to him is the truth); he maintained that there were no Soviet military personnel in Ethiopia at all. I knew that he was not giving me the facts, and he knew that I knew that he was not giving me the facts. But this was not a disillusionment for me. I was familiar enough with Soviet policy to realise that when the Politburo votes to tell the world that there are no Soviet military personnel in Ethiopia, then all the spokesmen for the Soviet Union give that statement, whether it's true or not.

CHARLTON: But why does that not also lead to something like a fundamental reappraisal of your attitude towards the Soviet Union? To see it, as many people have seen it since Lenin's revolution, as an incorrigible enemy, incapable of reassurance?

PRESIDENT CARTER: I don't have any disillusionments about the Soviets' ultimate goals which were expressed by Khruschev and others: 'We are going to bury the West, we're going to bury capitalism . . .' I think that is their ultimate goal. But at the same time, you know, I have to look at the Soviet Union and their policies as being in the best interests of their own people; and one of the major advantages to the Soviet Union is to maintain peace with the United States to the extent of avoiding a mutually destructive nuclear war. I also believe the Soviets are benefited whenever they can, with confidence, lower the level of military expenditure and improve the quality of life of their people. I also know that the Soviets want to put forward a good face, in order to improve their influence among the Third World nations. They don't *want* to be looked upon as a persistent aggressor; as one who abuses the peace; as one who persistently violates human rights. They want to put forward a good image. This is a very tangible political fact. It's not just an ephemeral idea.

CHARLTON: But was that not one of the reasons you were so shaken by what happened in Afghanistan?

PRESIDENT CARTER: Well, I had as that major goal of my Administration the conclusion of SALT II, and the immediate move toward much more drastic reductions – and I saw all this going out the window when the Soviets invaded Afghanistan. It was also abhorrent to me to see a powerful nation like the Soviets trying to subdue a freedom-loving people with military force.

When I was at Vienna with Brezhnev, he and I had already begun to discuss progressive steps to build upon SALT II. I proposed to him, for instance, that SALT II be implemented immediately we signed it, in its entirety, and not *wait* for Senate ratification. Secondly, that we have, over the five-year term of the treaty, a five per cent annual reduction compounded – which would have resulted in a forty or fifty per cent reduction *below* the SALT II limits. I proposed to him that we start immediately on the SALT III agreement and include, within that negotiation, the limited-range missiles in Europe, and that we implement a comprehensive test ban agreement and leave out the contentious factor (which was Great Britain's participation). The United Kingdom was being urged by the Soviets to have ten monitoring devices – just like us and the Soviets. I thought that three would have been a gracious plenty for Great Britain. But the Soviets refused. So I suggested to Brezhnev, 'Let's just leave out Great Britain and have a comprehensive test ban between *us*.' He was not willing to do any of those things. But at least, you know, I put forward the propositions. I gave them to him in my own handwriting, so that he might consider them over a period of time; and *all* of that disappeared, as an immediate prospect, with the Soviet invasion of Afghanistan.

IN REMINDING US, at the outset, of his mission to complete SALT II, 'the single most important challenge . . . which had required six-and-a-half years under three Presidents', President Carter made clear to us also his task. He was negotiating, not with the Russians alone, but with the Senate – and the Pentagon. The critique of his successor, President Reagan, would make much of the 'heritage of weakness' of the previous decade, but particularly the Carter years, and their undiscovery of American 'will' – that vital determinant which Clausewitz had defined as 'standing like an obelisk towards which the main streets of a town converge'. It was a charge that American strategic policy had failed to reconcile effectively the considerations of the diplomat and the soldier. The streets of the great American popular debate about SALT II, at the end of the 1970s did not always converge on Clausewitz's obelisk but, in the demonology of the protracted argument about arms control, have often led to the great five-sided citadel of American security – the Pentagon. How, in the light of the new balance of strategic forces emerging in consequence of the Soviet advances, did the soldier reconcile himself with the diplomat? The Chairman of the Joint Chiefs of Staff from 1978–82, advising President Carter and, for a time, President Reagan, was an Air Force officer, General David Jones.

GENERAL DAVID JONES: The Joint Chiefs have continuously supported good arms control negotiations. In many ways we're considered the moderates in the country and, at times, have surprised people by being such strong advocates of balanced and verifiable arms control. In all our deliberations we tried to avoid the political considerations, which tend to dominate arguments, and get into the specifics of what would create *stability*. Issues of verification were very important to us.

CHARLTON: Would you say the thinking of the Joint Chiefs about arms control has evolved in any particularly important way?

GENERAL JONES: I think as we got deeper into arms control came recognition of its increasing importance – that neither side could gain through nuclear war. It would be the most devastating thing mankind could imagine and there *must* be mutual interest by the two superpowers in reducing tensions and the likelihood of any conflict. You can make the point that arms control agreements have allowed continued modernisation and continued build-up; but that doesn't mean it hasn't been useful. There could have been a great deal *more* build-up. I hate to use the words 'arms race', as though we were two runners trying to keep up with one another on a level track competing in the same way. It is so complicated that it is just not susceptible to that simplification.

CHARLTON: Do you subscribe to the view of arms control that 'what is militarily significant is not negotiable and what is negotiable is not militarily significant'?

GENERAL JONES: No. I don't agree with that either. I'm never one to advocate that we have 'bargaining chips', or what I would call 'golden handcuffs' – meaning systems which you support only to give way in bargaining; or at the other extreme, certain things which are completely off-limits. I think everything ought to be on the table. To put something off the table because of problems of verification would be an appropriate thing. Otherwise, everything should be under consideration.

CHARLTON: What is the value of the process itself?

GENERAL JONES: One thing I don't think is fully recognised (especially when people are new to the process) is that the process is about as important as the results. SALT I, SALT II – what happened in limitations was quite moderate; but the fact that we were negotiating, that we were coming to some agreements, that each side had to take into consideration the concerns and views of the other side, tended to reduce the tension.

CHARLTON: What was your experience of how your opposite numbers in the Soviet Union saw the process of arms control?

GENERAL JONES: Well, one of the things I've advocated for many, many years is a dialogue between the senior military people of the two countries. When I met with Marshal Ogarkov, the Chief of the Soviet General Staff, in Vienna in 1979 (when I accompanied President Carter to the SALT II signing), that meeting was the first time that the two senior military leaders of the two countries had met since Marshal Zhukov and General George Marshall met right after the Second World War. And I found it a very useful meeting; not so much in the plenary sessions, but in the 'one-to-one' discussions that concerned a lot of misunderstandings and suspicions. Much of that could be eliminated if we had a good dialogue between the two. I found that, for example, in the discussion with Marshal Ogarkov, we could get to the specifics *without* all the dialectical rhetoric that one had in any discussion with Marshal Ustinov, who was Minister of Defence – a 'political' Marshal. With Marshal Ogarkov, who was a strong supporter of the Soviet system, of course, you could have a discussion *without* all the political terms coming in. The potential was what really impressed me rather than the specifics of the one meeting. I think, in a military discussion . . . 'camaraderie' is the wrong word, but there is an understanding among military people; they can 'talk' about these subjects.

CHARLTON: In historical terms, would you agree, it's going to be interesting to explain why, if the best military advice the Presidents are receiving in the 1970s into the 1980s is that a SALT II agreement is useful and has the Chiefs' blessing, the Senate felt unable to ratify it?

GENERAL JONES: I believe that if it hadn't been for outside circumstances the SALT II treaty would have been ratified. But things started to turn sour at that time, and then obviously when the Soviets invaded Afghanistan we had nothing to do but to drop the whole subject of SALT II. Our whole process is one of compromise. We don't expect to be able to dictate the terms of SALT II or SALT III, or whatever, but to have considerable influence. I think the Chiefs had considerable influence on SALT I. I *know* we had considerable influence in SALT II.

I found it very interesting that at the beginning of the present administration (President Reagan's), when very tough decisions were being made by the President whether or not to *abide* by SALT II, that the arguments *not* to undermine SALT II were by three military officers: the Secretary of State Al Haig, Admiral 'Bobby' Inman (who was sitting in as the acting head of the Central Intelligence Agency at that time) and myself as the Chairman of the Joint Chiefs of Staff. We all advocated that the US *not* take any steps to undermine SALT II. We took a lot of what we call 'flak' from our defence supporters during the SALT II debate in 1979. The people who were most supportive of defence were saying, 'Why are you, the Chiefs, supporting this fatally flawed treaty?' But we saw it as we continued to see it, modest but useful. We just tried to evaluate its effectiveness without any political considerations one way or the other.

CHARLTON: What was your approach to the unsettled controversy at the heart of all these matters – the nature of the Soviet state and your appreciation of their capacities and their purposes?

GENERAL JONES: It's not solved and, the way I see it, I don't think it can ever come to an agreement of what their intentions and purposes are. First, they want to be a true superpower. They want to be *recognised* as a true superpower. Arms control agreements tend to give them that image in the world of being an equal superpower. They are very defensive about their borders. We should not be surprised by the shooting down of the

Korean airliner, 007.[5] I wasn't. Every time I flew that route I knew that, if I strayed into the Soviet Union, at best I would be forced down and at worst I would be shot down. That's just a sort of obsession with the security of their land. Secondly, they want a series of buffer states around the Soviet Union. I don't think there is any chance they would have let Afghanistan turn neutral or hostile. They would have done something to get China – if they could have – when China left the Sino-Soviet bloc. But I think there is another sort of dilemma that faces the Soviet Union. They truly want to be a superpower and have more influence around the world ('control', maybe, more than influence), but they see that they have few tools other than military with which to influence what goes on in the world. They're clearly not a superpower from an economic standpoint. They're not even a major player in economic discussions. Marxism is less attractive to the world now than it was after World War II, when a lot of nations were flirting with it. So about the only aspect of their power that gives them a seat at the front table is *military* power. That's the one piece of power we would like to reduce – on both sides. We would like the military to be less of a factor in international relations.

CHARLTON: But does not the very fact that Communist ideology is no longer the recruiting sergeant for Communist influence it used to be, oblige us to realise that it is Soviet *military* power, and how others see its power, which fulfils that role now? Does that not increase the risk of Soviet 'adventure'?

GENERAL JONES: I think you could argue that. I think they would like to achieve clear-cut superiority from a military standpoint. They would clearly like to be in a dominant military position. But in a total sense of what one side can do to the other we're in reasonable parity. They have substantial advantages where we have to go thousands of miles to work with our allies. In other places that are far from the Soviet Union, we have a great advantage. In my home state of North Dakota there was an old saying that you could drown in a stream that had an *average* depth of three feet. Obviously that stream had deep parts and shallow parts. It is, I think, an apt analogy in the military balance between our two countries. We have areas where *they* have great advantages, areas where *we* have great advantages. Our greatest worry is that, if something happens, it may happen in an area where *they* have substantial advantage. But I think both of us have an interest beyond the political considerations. With each side having close to 25,000 nuclear weapons, there is a deep motivation to somehow figure out a less dangerous world.

HENRY KISSINGER HAD SEEN détente as the adaptation of containment to the new circumstances of nuclear parity. President Carter did not appear

---

[5] Flight 007, a civilian airliner shot down by Soviet fighters on 1 September 1983 while off course on a flight from Anchorage to Seoul, with the loss of 269 lives

to see the need for containment of Soviet expansion at all: as a strategic policy it had been 'based on an outdated view of the world'. Thus he spoke of America exercising 'mature restraint'. This reflected his belief that military power was becoming less and less useful as an instrument of policy in the Third World arena. Economic rather than political factors were setting the poorer nations of the South against the richer of the North. A new axis of conflict ran North and South around the world rather than East and West. These were the historical trends which, as President Carter said in 1977, 'have weakened the foundations on which American foreign policy had once stood – a belief that Soviet expansion was almost inevitable and that it must be contained.'

But a year later Jimmy Carter was saying: 'The persistent and increasing military involvement of the Soviet Union and Cuba in Africa could deny this hopeful vision.' The episode in the Horn of Africa, in Ethiopia, clearly strengthened the critics of détente and of Carter's 'mature restraint'. They maintained that the policy had rested on the questionable assumption that the Soviet Union would be restrained other than by Soviet assessments of American power and resolve. Soviet actions in Africa had returned a verdict on both. In response to events and to their consequences in the Carter years, the coalition of adversaries of arms control, on both left and right in America, emerged even more forcefully than in Kissinger's time. The arms control negotiations became indeed 'victim and orphan' of the new Soviet actions and changing American attitudes to the nature of the Soviet state.

HAROLD BROWN: I think what happened was US public dissatisfaction with a perceived shift of the military balance in a direction less favourable to the United States – this was one element. It included the results of the Vietnam War which, although a conventional non-nuclear war of an insurgency kind, was one that the United States had lost; and that contributed to this public attitude. So also, I think, did the build-up in Soviet strategic capability.

A second element, I think, was a movement – on the left, largely, and in intellectual circles – which was dissatisfied with arms control on the grounds that it merely legitimised a continued build-up of strategic forces on both sides. That was not confined to the left. Candidate Reagan said it, and President Reagan in fact still says it. But it did strike a responsive note in the public. The response that arms control had allowed a balanced build-up, and prevented the US from being disadvantaged, was undercut by charges that the US *was* being disadvantaged because of, for example, the 'throw-weight' disparity.[6]

From the left primarily, and from intellectuals also more generally, came

[6] The controversy embraced, ever since the first SALT treaty in 1972, by Senator Jackson concerning the capacities of the 'big' Soviet missile for first strike

the statement that nuclear deterrence was itself immoral, preventing war by threatening massive retaliation which would inevitably (or very likely) involve the destruction of tens of millions of ordinary people on each side. This, of course, during the early 1980s, received additional impetus from the analysis of the Pastoral Letter of the American Catholic bishops; but that, I think, was one of the more thoughtful elements in such an undercutting of deterrence. There were other responses, including Freeze movements and anti-nuclear marches; and on the right, arguments that the United States should not be satisfied with *deterring* a nuclear war by threatening to incinerate a hundred million Soviets. It should be prepared to *win* a nuclear war.

ALL THESE ARGUMENTS, including the last, were forcefully exposed in the Carter Administration. With the adoption of what was known as PD 59 (Presidential Directive 59), President Carter made the first avowed American retreat from the doctrine of 'mutual assured destruction' since Robert McNamara had become convinced in the 1960s that 'MAD' was an inescapable reality and the foundation of nuclear deterrence. By the time of the Carter Presidency two decades later, there was a progressive loss of confidence in McNamara's early hopes that there was a general strategic enlightenment to which all rational actors on the awful nuclear stage would conform. By then, also, the remarkable advances in the accuracy with which missiles could be flown to their targets, together with the gathering belief that the Soviet Union had never shared the Western concept of deterrence, introduced new calculations. It remained an imperative of Marxist-Leninist ideology that war was an instrument of policy from which nuclear weapons could not be exempt. In which case, did the United States have any choice other than to regard 'fighting and winning' a nuclear war in a more traditional perspective? General William Odom was an important contributor to the American judgment of Soviet policy and intentions, in the Pentagon as Assistant Chief of Intelligence and now as Director of the National Security Agency.

GENERAL WILLIAM ODOM: I see the Soviets building a very large force structure – as effective as they can make it – in order to affect the *political* climate in the East-West political competition. I would not impute to the Soviets a desire to use those weapons, to go to war. But the one thing they will not do to avoid it is to shrink from an essentially offensive political and military strategy in the world.
CHARLTON: Now, General, I don't want you to voice a treasonable utterance about a former Commander-in-Chief . . . but when President Carter said that neither side was able to manipulate nuclear weapons for political purposes, that would not be your judgment?
ODOM: No, I did not share that view with him. Nor did I think, *do* I think, President Carter held that view at all times.

CHARLTON: What makes you say that?

ODOM: Because under his administration (at least at the level of official policy) there was a more explicit shift away from 'assured destruction' in our policy than at any time since World War II.

CHARLTON: You mean the counter-force options ... like Presidential Directive 59?

ODOM: I mean Presidential Directive 41, which said that civil defence, like other strategic defence, is part of the overall balance – and once you say that *defence* is part of the balance, you have abandoned 'assured destruction'. Also the telecommunications presidential directive, which required communications, command and control capability for all levels of war, even large-scale nuclear war. And then you mentioned PD 59, which was really only a final step down a series of policy steps that marked a rather significant transformation.

CHARLTON: But these counter-force doctrines, which you've just ...

ODOM: I didn't call them counter-force doctrines, you did. Counter-force doctrine? That's part of the Ptolemaic view of the solar system!

CHARLTON: I apologise. How should one describe them?

ODOM: Well, using nuclear weapons in support of military – of war – objectives. In the event deterrence fails, how you would use them to succeed in operational objectives, to your advantage. President Reagan essentially broke up this polarisation between the 'mutual assured destruction' proponents and the war-fighting proponents. He has them seriously debating the issue of strategic defence once more. I think that is quite an extraordinary achievement. I took a great deal of heat during the Carter Administration for being a proponent of civil defence – and for some of these presidential directives you're talking about. It's delightful to see someone succeed in forcing people to recognise some of the moral, philosophical and objective paradoxes in the notion that it is evil to do things that would cause more people to survive in the event deterrence failed.

WE HAVE GENERAL ODOM'S WORD for it that this period must be seen as 'marking a rather significant transformation' in American strategic thinking; a period which reopens the paths to serious consideration of strategic *defence* and – in the next administration – to President Reagan's 'Defence Initiative', 'Star Wars'. The new policy steps, embodied in President Carter's Presidential Directives 41 and 59, accommodated new weapons developments and reflected the aroused concern during the Carter Administration about Soviet intentions. The President was addressing, as his predecessors had done, the central question: what deters the Soviet Union? More precisely, what was the ability of nuclear weapons to deter aggression if stability, expressed as mutual assured destruction, continued to be acknowledged?

Robert McNamara had wished, at first, to provide President Kennedy with an array of nuclear threats and warnings which would be an alternative to the extremes of doing nothing and the unimaginable catastrophe of ordering the prompt deaths of many tens of millions of people in all-out nuclear exchanges. In this particular respect (*pace* General Odom), President Carter's PD 59 represented a return to McNamara's earlier ideas which, it was suggested, the advances in nuclear technique now made more plausible. PD 59 presupposed the possibility of 'limited nuclear exchanges' against precise military and industrial targets in the manner of traditional military exchanges in the past, in order to reinforce the deterring threat of nuclear weapons. These were new shadows on the cave wall. They reflected 'thinking about the unthinkable' – the mirror image of Soviet policy. When President Carter signed Presidential Directive 59 into existence in 1980, what had he intended to convey?

PRESIDENT CARTER: Some of the motives behind these presidential directives are still highly secret. But there were two overall considerations that I think I can give you. One is that we had a new relationship with China, whereas in the past we always considered ourselves as being required to prepare for two-and-a-half wars – to fight against the Soviets, to fight against the Chinese, and then to fight some small regional conflict that might erupt in the Middle East or Central America or somewhere. After we normalised relations with China, it became obvious that it was highly unlikely, even with the greatest stretch of the imagination, that we would go to war with China. That was one of the factors involved. The other one was to target our nuclear strike locations in order to avoid concentrating on population centres, and specifically to destroy the military and industrial capabilities of the Soviet Union.

CHARLTON: Raymond Aron, the French political philosopher, used to call this sort of thing 'strategic fiction'. Is that a term you recognise or agree with?

PRESIDENT CARTER: Well, you know it wasn't nearly as profound as some philosophers or military analysts say. It was an adjustment.

CHARLTON: But were you not seeking, in putting PD 59 forward, to replace 'mutual assured destruction', the doctrine of MAD?

PRESIDENT CARTER: Not really. I think that, if you'll let me use my expression, 'mutual assured *vulnerability*' still persists. I've forgotten the exact figures, but if we'd unleashed even one of our Trident submarines and destroyed just the 'Soviet military and industrial capabilities that would entail, there would still be tens of millions of people killed. I think the Soviets recognised that they could not ever with impunity launch an attack on our country, and that's the essence of it.

CHARLTON: But you do not say 'destruction', 'mutual assured destruction'?

PRESIDENT CARTER: Well, you can say it if you like. But I think 'vulnerability' is a more accurate word because the motivation for both sides is not the destruction of the other country, but to make sure that the other country is *vulnerable* – and recognises its vulnerability. So I think 'mutal assured vulnerability' is a more accurate expression. This has always been the basis – still is the basis – for the arsenals that we both have. Any sort of *radical* departure from this premise is an extremely disturbing factor; both in the relationship between the two nations (mutual trust must be engendered and maintained) and in the prospect for arms control.

CHARLTON: But was PD 59 meant to send certain signals to the Soviet Union?

PRESIDENT CARTER: Not really. This was not a presidential directive that was publicised. It was for our own military forces and was evolved over a period of a couple of years. It was a very careful analysis about how to use any level of nuclear attack in the most effective way. Of course, if we launched our entire nuclear arsenal the destruction would probably encompass the entire earth.

THE PRESIDENT'S TONE CONCERNING PD 59 seems almost deprecatory. Whether the statesman does indeed consider such scenarios to be doctrine, or whether they point more to an attitude, is part of the strange mental universe of deterrence which, if it cannot convince, cannot be refuted. But the more explicit speculations about limited nuclear war have played their part in animating the Peace and the Freeze movements in the West. Here is the genesis of some at least of the factors which have led President Reagan to respond with his 'Star Wars' proposal and say, in effect, 'You are afraid of nuclear war – I will protect you!'

Two years after he had gone to the White House believing that the West had had an 'inordinate fear of Communism', President Carter said (in 1978) that, to the Russians, 'Détente seems to mean a continuing struggle for advantages in which the Soviet Union apparently sees military power and military assistance as the best means of expanding their influence.' Jimmy Carter described his policy for a stable relationship with the Soviet Union as 'competition and co-operation'. But, undermined by Soviet actions, the path of co-operation – whose principal symbol was arms control – was rapidly breaking up. It remained for one event in particular, the Soviet invasion of Afghanistan, to eliminate it.

PRESIDENT CARTER: I have always been convinced up until this moment that we could have gotten SALT II ratified – had the Soviets not invaded Afghanistan.

CHARLTON: When that invasion comes, towards the end of 1979, we find you saying this: 'My opinion of the Russians has changed more drastically in the last week than in the previous two and a half years.' Can you amplify that? What did you mean?

PRESIDENT CARTER: Up until then the Soviets had basically used surrogates to carry out their aggression or their use of military force to expand their influence – in Vietnam, and also with the Cubans in Angola, and to some lesser degree in Ethiopia. And here the Soviets, in Afghanistan, reverted to what I thought was a very counter-productive use of their own military forces in an adjacent country, one of the satellite nations, Afghanistan. They brought on themselves the condemnation of the entire world. And I think they not only opened up for themselves a much higher degree of worldwide condemnation, which weakened the Soviets among the Third World countries, but cast out of the window the benefits of good relations with us – and also the amplification of the SALT II treaty. So I think they just made a horrible mistake.

CHARLTON: Why do you think they did?

PRESIDENT CARTER: Why do I think they did it? I think misjudgment. I have read some analyses, even from the Soviet Union, that indicate that the Soviets think it might have been a misjudgment. But who knows what goes on in the secret chambers there? I think they thought that they could rapidly subdue the Afghans – which flies in the face of historical fact. I think they also looked at the troubled region in the Persian Gulf, Iran and Iraq, as a possible or ultimate target for them to gain access to warm southern ports and to capture the oil supplies in that region.

CHARLTON: But doesn't that only lend credence to Brezhnev's reported statement to the Warsaw Pact meeting in 1973 that the correlation of forces had moved sufficiently in their favour to allow him to take that risk[7]?

PRESIDENT CARTER: Yes, I think that does add credence to what he said. But it still doesn't confirm that what he said was accurate – because I think the Soviets are worse off now because of the invasion of Afghanistan.

CHARLTON: You say you could have got SALT II through the Senate, had it not been for Afghanistan. But I wonder whether you would not agree, in retrospect, that your twin relationship of co-operation and competition with the Soviet Union was disappearing even before the Soviet invasion of Afghanistan? We find Senator Nunn, for example, saying in a speech in 1979 that SALT II was in trouble by then, 'with a vote of only nine to six in favour of it in the Senate Foreign Relations Committee'. The Senate was voting to increase defence expenditures at that time above the requests your administration was asking for. It only remained therefore for the invasion of Afghanistan to eliminate your approach altogether?

PRESIDENT CARTER: No one can be sure what would have happened if they had not invaded Afghanistan. I'm still convinced that I'm right when I tell you what I did. Remember, too, that Sam Nunn's statements are not

---

[7] In Prague the East Germans had expressed misgivings about Kissinger's détente and whether it could get out of hand. Brezhnev's reported answer was: 'Trust us, comrades. By 1985, as a consequence of what we are achieving by détente, we will have achieved most of our objectives . . . the shift in the correlation of forces will be such that, come 1985, we will be able to exert our will wherever we need to.'

incompatible. One of the ways to have SALT II approved by defence-minded senators, like Sam Nunn, is to increase the defence budget. You know, there's always a matter of jockeying, and negotiating, within the Senate when they know that you have to get two-thirds of the vote. Then people who have special projects, and like a much higher level of defence expenditure than I had advocated, used this as a bargaining chip.

CHARLTON: In the first three years of your government you were facing not just the Soviet military build-up, creating increasing doubt and unease. There was the Cuban and Soviet intervention in the Horn of Africa, and the loss of four countries to governments which were less friendly to the United States than their predecessors had been: Afghanistan (in 1978, before the Soviet invasion); South Yemen; the Sandinistas in Nicaragua (the overthrow of Somoza); and the Shah in Persia. Now all of these were considered defeats in terms of American influence. I wonder whether that does not put what Nunn had said in a rather different light? That your 'twin-track' strategy of co-operation and competition was running on the rocks – even before the invasion of Afghanistan?

PRESIDENT CARTER: I don't agree that all of those were characterised as American defeats, even then. Over a period of time there had been notable Soviet defeats as well; and, you know, there is a constant give-and-take and jockeying back and forth, some victories and some setbacks. But I still have no doubt that, because of the merits of the case, the SALT II treaty *would* have been ratified. I think this is corroborated to some degree by the fact that President Reagan himself has announced that he is abiding by the SALT II treaty; and, of course, he is heavily influenced by many of those who were opposed to the treaty (or professed to be opposed to it) back in 1979.

WHAT THEN IS THE POSSIBILITY of America finding in its relations with the Soviet Union a middle way which is also a balanced, stable and continuing policy? Both Henry Kissinger's détente, and President Carter's theory of that relationship as partly competitive and partly co-operative, had tried in their different ways to do this. Neither could be sustained. Both were held to be failures by the end of the decade of the 1970s, President Carter's in the backwash of Soviet actions and the rising wave of anti-Soviet feeling in America which carried President Reagan to the White House.

We might recall Henry Kissinger's review of a diplomacy of which he was the principal architect: 'While we made our share of mistakes, the fundamental assault on détente came from Moscow, not from Washington.' In his turn, what did President Carter believe to be the Soviet contribution to the decline in support for his own passionate concern – arms control?

PRESIDENT CARTER: I think there was a *great* contribution on the part of the Soviets to the decline of arms control. Their Afghanistan invasion set it back several years, and I think that President Reagan's 'Star Wars' proposal is likely to set it back an equal period of time.

CHARLTON: Do you regret, though, that you didn't go on with SALT yourself right to the very end, take it to the country, risk everything?

PRESIDENT CARTER: No. I did the best I could. The only thing that I could do with SALT II was to prevent it being defeated; and as you know, it was not defeated. I requested from the Senate majority leader, Senator Byrd, that the treaty be held in the breast of the Foreign Relations Committee of the Senate, not be brought to the floor for a vote – because it was obvious, after the Afghan invasion, that if it had been brought to the Senate floor it would have been defeated and therefore rejected. It is still in the breast of the Foreign Relations Committee.

CHARLTON: No regrets that you didn't fight the election on it, or something like that?

PRESIDENT CARTER: No, I don't think so; it was impossible. Because of their persistent attacks on the people of Afghanistan, the Soviets were so condemned by me and by the American people by the time the 1980 election came along that it would not have been possible to promote better relations between us.

CHARLTON: Would you agree that, when you came to office, conservatism was on the march in the United States – intellectually, politically? After all, your own victory was a victory over some of the traditional American liberals.

PRESIDENT CARTER: I've always looked upon myself as a conservative in some ways. I am a military-trained man. I always believed in a strong defence, and we had a constant build-up in our military budget each year above inflation rate – and induced our NATO allies to make the same commitment. I have always believed in a balanced budget and in very tight fiscal constraints. I have always believed that the federal government should play a lesser role as compared to the state and local governments. I have also believed that our free enterprise system should be greatly deregulated and the highest level of competition prevail. So I think some of those elements would be characterised, generally, as conservative. As you undoubtedly know, if you've studied the fiscal records of our country, the eight years before I came in was a time of great *reductions* in our defence budgets. This wasn't caused by the attitude of Presidents Nixon and Ford, but because of substantial reductions each year below the presidential budgets, forced by the Congress – in reaction to Vietnam.

JIMMY CARTER'S CREDO WAS NOT attended by good fortune. He had come to office when 'the great arsenal of democracy', as Roosevelt had called it, was bestirring itself amid the heated partialities and prejudices which had marked the 1970s. He could not sustain the confidence or loyalty of an America which found 'mature restraint' less convincing than regaining its old ebullience. The impotence with which the United States watched the long imprisonment of its embassy staff in Teheran, as hostages of the revolution which overthrew the Shah, may be said to mark the end of one design of American foreign policy – and the Soviet invasion of Afghanistan the beginning of another. The divisions within the Carter Administration – the general tone of indecisiveness which it set when it was faced with increasing antagonism and competition with the Russians, the frustrations attributed to the decline in American power (which President Carter had actually reversed) – assured the triumph of its conservative critics and paved the way for President Reagan.

President Carter had tried to expand the number and the scope of arms control agreements. But he doubts America's willingness to accept genuine equality – 'what we define as equality is almost inevitably going to be superiority'. And when each superpower possesses today some 25,000 nuclear weapons, what is superiority? We arrive at the challenge to this impasse in thought entered by President Reagan's Strategic Defence Initiative, 'Star Wars'.

★ 5 ★
DEFENCE IN SPACE:

President Reagan Moves the Goalposts

A LONGING TO RECAPTURE THE PAST has a history of its own in the American political tradition. John Dos Passos wrote of this national nostalgia, 'In times of change and danger, when there is a quicksand of fear under men's reasoning, a sense of continuity with generations gone before can stretch like a lifeline across the scary present . . .'. President Reagan was not elected because he offered America pessimism, but because he embodied in his feelings and beliefs the reassurance of old certainties.

Among the historical certainties which have made America a society of well-fulfilled promises has been the vitality and exuberance of its applied technology. American technology – democratising its ideas and innovations from Edison's electric light to Ford's motor car and the present-day computer – has spread out all over the atlas, transforming modern living everywhere. The President's Strategic Defence Initiative ('Star Wars') speech of 23 March 1983 draws heavily on faith in this tradition. President Reagan called upon the scientific community to: 'give us the means of rendering nuclear weapons impotent and obsolete with the ultimate goal of eliminating the threat posed by strategic nuclear missiles'.

But that threat has formed the architecture of strategic equilibrium and nuclear deterrence. The President has moved the goalposts. We have come full circle from the great debate initiated by Robert McNamara in the 1960s – which led to the virtual renunciation of defence against nuclear retaliation. Whether the 'Star Wars' concept will prove helpful or harmful in building a more stable world may already be academic. Defence against the ballistic missile has already acquired a self-interested impetus. We do not have the luxury of waiting – possibly for many years – for a scientific verdict on its practicality; 'Star Wars' is politics now.

The President himself is a figure of central importance to its future. His sentiments are in step with the platform on which he was elected. This called for an overall military and technological superiority over the Soviet

Union, and included the injunction 'to pursue the vigorous research and development of an effective anti-ballistic missile system, such as is already in hand in the Soviet Union – as well as more modern ABM technologies'.

In the early days of his administration the President put this question before a number of scientists. Among the most influential was the dark, brooding intelligence of the brilliant Hungarian emigré who, thirty years before, had fought and won the seminal argument with Robert Oppenheimer over whether America should build the hydrogen bomb. In the course of several meetings with President Reagan in 1982, Dr Edward Teller played a major part in stimulating an interest, apparently of longer standing, and in encouraging the President to believe that a novel way might be found to replace the bleak presumptions of 'mutual assured destruction' which have dominated the superpower rivalry for a third of this century.

EDWARD TELLER: A few weeks after he became Governor of California, I believe in 1966, I went to see him and invited him to come to visit our weapons laboratory in Livermore, California. He came. He listened carefully; not to a highly technical presentation, but to one that must have contained a host of completely novel ideas. He asked maybe ten or twelve questions which clearly showed that he followed – that he comprehended. Indeed, he was the only Governor who ever visited our laboratory.

I know that, in connection with the Strategic Defence Initiative, he had been discussing it for many months, *before* he asked his famous question on 23 March 1983: 'Isn't it better to save lives than to avenge them?'. Roosevelt, I know (I lived through that period and I have good information), made his decision about our going ahead with the atomic bomb in practically no time at all. He shot from the hip. He attacked. Reagan is incomparably more cautious – no matter what the *New York Times* tried to say. I cannot go into details, but it must have been clear to the President in 1966 that to emphasise defence was my desire. Not my 'plan', because none of us then saw a good way to realise this desire. But by 1983, he clearly knew that there was not only a will but a way.

CHARLTON: So how should we see the context in which the SDI was brought forward and made, as the Administration says, 'central' to its strategy?

TELLER: The policy of the West is to preserve peace. We tried to do it by deterrence – because on the other side, in the East, there is an expansionist, imperialistic power. Peace was to be preserved by the obvious means of *deterrence*: the menace of retaliation. It was called 'mutual assured destruction', MAD, and I don't think any of us liked it from the very beginning. It has been not quite morally acceptable; not to me, not (I believe) to any reasonable person. There seemed to be no alternative. Now an alternative *has* emerged. We find in our developing technology more and more possibilities of real defence. Not with the idea and, I would certainly say, not with the assurance of *complete* protection, but with the idea that defence can make the result of aggression doubtful – we hope highly doubtful. And, because the Kremlin is as power-hungry as the Nazis ever were (they are much more cautious), we believe they can be deterred by an effective defence. Thereby aggression and retaliation will not only become morally bankrupt but also bankrupt in a strict technical sense. This is what made the Strategic Defence Initiative, and an emphasis, generally, on defence, both possible and necessary.

CHARLTON: What do you say to those who consider that 'mutual assured destruction' is not a doctrine, it is a fact of life, the inescapable reality of the nuclear age?

TELLER: It *seemed* inescapable – now through detailed technical discussions we find it is *not* inescapable. It failed, because throughout history (certainly throughout recent history) it has been clearly proved that a governmental policy which is not supported by the will of the people is not going to succeed.

DR EDWARD TELLER'S SUMMARY of his views to President Reagan offered compelling political inducements. By then the Catholic bishops in America had added their moral concern about nuclear deterrence to the popular ferments of the Peace and Freeze movements. Large-scale political demonstrations against the Cruise and Pershing missiles – the West's response to the Soviet Union's attempt to tilt the balance on the continent by introducing in large numbers a new first-strike weapon, the SS–20 – had been a struggle for the soul of Europe. In the unremitting competition with the Russians, strategic defence – to be developed from the new X-ray and *non-nuclear* laser technologies – held out the prospect of that popular support which had been grudgingly given, or even withheld, from competitive increases in the vast destructive power of the nuclear arsenals.

In addition, Dr Teller's advice was that *mutual assured survival*, rather than 'mutual assured destruction', could be installed on terms favourable to the West. To the still uncertain extent that it is really serious political business, the 'Star Wars' concept could undo whatever benefit the Russians believe has accrued to them from their strategic modernisation programme of the past twenty years. They could be contemplating the obsolescence of their huge land-based missile force before the end of this century. It is clear that, given their assessment of the state of the Soviet economy, the Americans believe the Russians will be at a competitive disadvantage; if not in the science itself, then in the applications of that science. What then is open to the Soviet Union to do about 'Star Wars'? President Reagan's Defence Secretary, Caspar Weinberger.

CASPAR WEINBERGER: I think there are a number of things they could do. They could certainly agree – to their own very great advantage economically as well as militarily – to vastly lower levels of offensive armament. This would enable both of us to maintain deterrence, but at considerably lower cost and at considerably less threat and risk. So far they haven't shown the slightest interest in doing that.

The SALT agreements (SALT I and SALT II) unfortunately did not *reduce* arms at all. They authorised an increase in arms. The Soviets, without violating SALT II, increased their numbers of nuclear warheads by an enormous extent during the period since that agreement was signed (even though it was not formally ratified or enacted, so to speak). They *do* need a respite. They can't feed themselves: their agriculture is in very bad shape; their economy is not such that will produce any kind of quality of life for the individual citizen. You and I would not be able to stand that kind of life for more than a couple of weeks.

But without any public opinion, without any requirement to change the heavy emphasis on the military, devoting at least eighteen to nineteen per cent of their Gross National Product to the military (probably a lot more, because they're able to hide it in their closed society), they are under no pressure or compulsion to change policies. That is a worrisome thing because democracies are governed, as they should be, by public opinion. We are, naturally, very impatient. So the Soviets and their dictatorship can always out-wait us in any kind of negotiation, knowing that we are very eager to reach agreement and that time is on their side.

CHARLTON: You say that they need a respite. Do you subscribe to the belief that they face, perhaps, a turning point in their history?

WEINBERGER: They may. It's hard to see that they recognise that, because they have not indicated any change in their basic policies going back many, many years – long before the Communists took over. There are a lot of the basic Soviet – basic Russian – foreign policy goals that have not changed at all. I don't think they recognise, or are prepared to recognise yet, that they do face any kind of turning point; and I don't see any real change, or any real possibility of modification of their basic policies.

CHARLTON: In other words, 'retreat' by them is seen by you as very unlikely.

WEINBERGER: Very unlikely indeed.

CHARLTON: They will not sacrifice their world position for domestic reform?

WEINBERGER: Well, not only not sacrifice their position. They will do everything they can to increase their military capabilities and along with it everything else.

CHARLTON: Why is the existing concept of deterrence proving inadequate (or likely to prove inadequate) as you see it?

WEINBERGER: It is based on the idea that both sides are perfectly safe if both sides are perfectly vulnerable. That's all right, perhaps, if you have *total agreement*; not only as to the concept, as to the strategy, but also its execution. The Anti-Ballistic Missile Treaty, and the concept of 'mutual assured destruction', is based on the idea that there will, first of all, be equality (or very close to it) or 'parity' on *offensive* systems; and that there will be no activity on the *defensive* side, except the relatively ineffective kinds specifically authorised by the treaty – that is, a ground-based system which is around fifty per cent effective. Unfortunately, neither of those assumptions has been adhered to by the Soviet Union. They have violated the ABM treaty with the construction of the radar at Krasnoyarsk, which cannot have any direct application except as part of a strategic defence capability. . . .

CHARLTON: That bears no other interpretation?

WEINBERGER: No, I don't think so at all. I understand all the arguments the Soviets make, but you don't build a radar like that for any of those purposes. You can acquire that kind of capability far more simply and in different locations. The other thing is that the ABM treaty itself – and almost everybody seems to have forgotten this – called for an early meeting to discuss and agree upon very substantial *reductions* in offensive weapons. And that never took place.

CHARLTON: There was a considerable opposition to the ABM treaty of 1972. Some people in the United States believed it was a 'historic mistake'. Mr Reagan criticised it at the time. What was your own view? What view do you take of it now?

WEINBERGER: I had the view at the time that the idea of relying on promises by the Soviet Union, and on the hope that they would bring about major reductions in offensive weapons, was perhaps not well founded. Then, as the developments of the years progressed, and watching their increasing research into 'defence' and their potential capabilities, my feeling became very strong that we should, at the very least, hedge against any kind of major, massive 'break-out' by the Soviet Union on the defensive side. If there is adherence to the ABM treaty, *if* there is observation of it, it could provide a basis for maintaining the peace. But when there are violations on *two sides*, on the side of offence and of defence, then continued inaction on our part (they spend as much on defensive systems as they do on offence now) could put us all in very substantial peril. We cannot ignore what they're doing in violation of the ABM treaty both specifically and in the broad concept. They are acquiring a major defensive capability. They are increasing their enormous capability on the offensive side.

CHARLTON: What role will your Strategic Defence Initiative play if you wish to *compel* the Soviet Union to make these reductions? Presumably they will answer that they need the edge they possess (in the numbers of offensive missiles) in order to cope with any such development?

WEINBERGER: That overlooks the question of how the West is going to cope with the Soviet strategic defence – on which they have been working for seventeen years – whereas we have, practically speaking, just started. Strategic defence, I think, can play a very major role both in enhancing deterrence and ultimately (if we are successful – and we don't know if we will be) in removing a lot of the threat and the shadow of terror that nuclear weapons, possessed by the Soviets, have cast over the world.

THIS UNDERLINES THE EMOTIONAL appeal of the 'Star Wars' concept – the prospect of liberating humanity from the incapacitating threat of nuclear bombardment. Unlike the last time strategic defence was an issue in the United States – at the end of the 1960s – there is an absence today of that feeling of generosity with which Robert McNamara felt the Soviet Union might be treated. McNamara's hopes were that, once the US had so unequivocally overhauled the dramatic strategic advantage that the Soviet Union acquired by being first into space with an intercontinental rocket carrying Sputnik, time and technology would bring about 'a convergence' of ideas – that a plateau of nuclear sufficiency would then have been established beyond which the Russians would not wish to go. The generosity was symbolised by McNamara's dismantling of the (then probably superior) American ballistic missile defences in search of agreement. With the Carter years came explicit concern that the Soviet Union did not believe the concept of military advantage had been made obsolete by parity in the nuclear weapon – Harold Brown's thesis of continual, uninterrupted 'building'. Today the men of influence in the Reagan Administration are persuaded that there is a permanent dialectic of the two contending political wills. I asked a scientist who for decades has played a pivotal role in the nuclear era about his faith in the innovative, aggressive exploitation of technology rather than diplomacy to save the West from nuclear war.

EDWARD TELLER: Let me change your question. I would call it the *defensive* exploitation of technology, not aggressive exploitation. I don't underestimate diplomacy. Diplomacy involving, say, the United States and France is difficult enough, requires lots of ingenuity, and has rewards. But diplomacy in discussions with people whose clearly pursued purpose is to use diplomacy to break agreements (secretly or openly, whenever it suits their purpose), and to strive for agreements which are not equitable – I believe that that kind of diplomacy has to be handled with very great care. I do not give priority to technology. I just claim that the big changes of our times, in civilian life as well as in military surroundings, turn on technology – not because we want it so, but because technology usually changes more rapidly than people's conception of science and technology can follow.

CHARLTON: And so the vital necessity, as you see it, of maintaining a 'technological edge' for the West rules out the concession to the Soviet Union of that equality they are always seeking, and demanding, as an instrument of policy from the West?

TELLER: The Soviets demand equality; they seek superiority. Indeed, equality is a mirage. In a rapidly developing field – which is hard to follow even if you know all the details – where you may, with great diligence, know all the details on our side, but where we are completely denied the inside data on where the Soviets stand – how do you know whether you are 'equal' or not? If you try to make sure that you are not ahead of them, you are apt to make sure that they are ahead of us. I believe that 'equality' is a word of beautiful sound, of great moral depth, and of no practical applicability whatsoever.

DR TELLER'S DISMISSAL OF the principle of equality identifies also the dead-end in the theory of arms control, where the condition of agreement is that both sides accept the same objective: stability through equality. Since the first SALT agreement in 1972, which was provisional in character, neither side has been able to agree in their calculations of equality. The experience of years of arms control since then has been described by Hal Sonnenfeldt (one of Henry Kissinger's aides in those first negotiations in Moscow): 'What is militarily significant is not negotiable and what is negotiable is not militarily significant.' There are ten to twelve thousand strategic nuclear weapons in the Soviet offensive arsenal today, aimed at perhaps one hundred American cities. They may grow to fifteen to twenty thousand in the next ten years. Millions of human lives on either side are thrown into this equation. The Strategic Defence Initiative has been put forward as a moral and a practical answer. The claims of 'deliverance' made for the concept have, however, met with widespread disbelief or scepticism from reputable scientists. Whether the President and his advisers have allowed an initial enthusiasm to go further than the laws of nature (or the history of conflict) will allow awaits another – and a later – judgment. Dr George Keyworth – one of the younger generation of American physicists and a protégé of Edward Teller – was Science Adviser to the President of the United States at the time, and he helped to draft President Reagan's 'Star Wars' speech.

GEORGE KEYWORTH: I think that the SDI is the missing catalyst to achieving success in arms control for a very fundamental reason. It is the threat of a first strike (that is, the loss of our own retaliatory capabilities) that has led to the arms race. Now, with the Strategic Defence Initiative, even in its first stages, the feasibility of a first strike is immediately removed. We no longer need these gigantic arsenals. The ICBM (the intercontinental ballistic missile) is, in large measure, no longer a practical weapon to initiate war. Here is the catalyst to achieve not a ten per cent reduction in ICBMs, but to drastically diminish the 1400 missiles the Soviet Union possesses today to merely enough to maintain a strong deterrent. This could be dozens, could be a hundred.

CHARLTON: But in order to be successful the SDI *needs*, does it not, a reduction in the offensive missiles of the Soviet Union?

KEYWORTH: I don't think so at all, and I think incidentally that that is a very important point to remember. As Paul Nitze, our most experienced arms negotiator, has pointed out time and time again, there must be two criteria satisfied by the SDI – one, that it be cost-effective. Now that's really very simple: what it means is that a unit of defence must be cheaper than a unit of offence. Defence *must* be cheaper than the Soviet Union simply building more missiles. And secondly, that it must be 'survivable' and thus not invite a first-strike attack. Now if those criteria are met – and we believe that we can meet those criteria, after we have done some more research – then I think the question is straightforwardly answered. With defence being cheaper than offence, you can destroy the force size that the Soviet Union possesses today, and you can in principle deter the Soviet Union from multiplying it by a factor of ten, five, or any other number.

CHARLTON: But that must remain an untested proposition, perhaps for many years to come. How do you meet the critique of men such as Hans Bethe and Richard Garwin (whose credentials, you would agree, are acknowledged and include the achievement of the American H-bomb) when they say this:

> On the basis of our technical analysis and our assessment of the most likely response of the Soviet Union, we conclude that the pursuit of the President's programme would inevitably stimulate a large increase in the Russian strategic offensive forces.

KEYWORTH: I think that both Dr Bethe and Dr Garwin have carried forth the arguments that surrounded the ABM treaty some ten or fifteen years ago. That was a very different era. It was far before the technology revolution that we are living with today. We have seen and examined very carefully a number of approaches that, we believe, offer us a very different opportunity – one that I do not believe they have addressed in detail. It goes back to that point of defence being cheaper than offence. If you can simply build more *defences* more cheaply than you can build more *offences*, then the ballistic missile is essentially an *obsolete* weapon. First, I believe we can do it. What is most important is that we should try. This is an era when technology is changing faster than the human imagination. I will go so far as to say that I believe we can demonstrate the feasibility of this endeavour even before this decade is out.

CHARLTON: Doesn't this mean, though, that the Soviet Union has to accept your version of what is expensive, what is costly?

KEYWORTH: Fortunately I am a scientist and not an accountant. Most certainly, when I talk about 'cheaper' I'm not talking about ten per cent – not even a factor of two. I am talking about such an *overwhelming* difference in the cost of defence and offence that there would be no question on that issue.

Let me offer an example. One of the approaches that we are pursuing is of a very large, very powerful, ground-based laser, which could penetrate the atmosphere and which could emanate perhaps ten to twenty pulses per second, or six to twelve hundred pulses per minute. Each of these pulses could destroy a ballistic missile. In other words, *one* laser (which we believe could be built within quite reasonable cost) could, in principle, defend the West against the entire Soviet ballistic missile fleet today. We are not talking about marginal balances. We are talking about radically new technologies.

CHARLTON: We have had roughly forty years' experience of the nuclear age and of nuclear weapons. Some would say that that divides itself into two halves – twenty years of inexperience and twenty years of experience. But what is common is that the nuclear *threat* has kept the peace.

KEYWORTH: I think it is important to look at the *trends* of the nuclear age, and the nature of the time today. I think that is exactly what President Reagan did. First, we must remember that we had essentially a first half, as you put it, in which the West possessed overwhelming military superiority. In the second half we have seen a continual erosion in the nature of nuclear stability. Let's examine exactly why that occurred. I think it was the introduction not so much of 'MIRVing' (of multiple nuclear weapons on a single missile), but rather of the so-called 'counter-force' targeting missiles, which became so accurate that you could literally imagine targeting the other side's retaliatory capability. Threatening that balance has led to the arms race that we live with – uncomfortably, I might add – today. If we look at the last twenty years in particular, what we see is a constant erosion in stability. I think those that look back and say we've had peace for forty years are missing the point. We should be looking at the trends. We should ask ourselves what the next forty years are going to be like.

CHARLTON: What were the actual circumstances in which the President made the speech of 23 March 1983? Nothing was really different in the world. Nothing had happened. The speech appeared to come out of the blue.

KEYWORTH: I think there is no question what was the stimulus. It was the fact that the President had just completed two years immersed in the complexities of modernising our own strategic forces and realising the limitations which his successors would confront on a curve of simply eroding nuclear stability. It is quite logical, I think, that the SDI proposal came at the conclusion of our two-year-long debate on strategic modernisation.

CHARLTON: Yet I've seen you quoted as saying that this was 'not a speech which came from the bottom up; it came from the top down . . .', which does not seem to argue that it received a widespread and careful analysis before it was made.

KEYWORTH: The President saw the need – better, I think, than anyone, and for the reasons I mention, of his successors not possessing sufficient tools with which to manage their challenges in the future. He saw the need to restore a stable balance and a desire to achieve an ultimate goal of drastically diminished reliance upon nuclear weapons. What made him decide that 'now' was the time to begin this initiative was the state of technology and the rate of progress, in the last few years, underlying those technologies.

HENRY KISSINGER HAD EXPRESSED his concern at more than one stage of the long negotiations with the Russians over SALT II (the treaty signed by President Carter but which is still unratified) that 'there seemed to be no conceptual basis for an agreement'. Upon President Reagan's election, his administration confronted the same difficulty at home – within America itself. The debate concerning the utility of arms control and the nature of nuclear deterrence had become increasingly acrimonious. It had become concentrated on the question of going ahead with a new, heavy American missile, MX, as a counter to the big Soviet missile, the SS–18.

In order to restore the necessary wide accord over how the United States was to look at strategic nuclear forces and their future development, the President appointed a Commission whose mandate was to try to close the gap that existed between the new administration and those in the political and defence community who had had a close association with Nixon and Kissinger's détente and SALT. The establishment of such a body was eloquent witness to the extent America had lost confidence in the enduring or sufficient quality of its own strategic analysis. The deliberations of the President's Commission on Strategic Forces were at the heart of what Dr Keyworth has described to us as President Reagan's two-year-long 'immersion in the complexities of modernising America's strategic forces'.

When the Commission reported, it appeared to confirm the 'retreat' from 'assured destruction' which had become more openly declared in President Carter's time. There was also a qualified endorsement of the opposition to the SALT agreements on the grounds that they had codified an American vulnerability (to the possibility of a Soviet first strike), based upon the Soviet advantage in large land-based missiles. This was the controversy which had set the tone of the strategic debate in the 1970s.

We have Dr Keyworth's opinion that it was logical the SDI should follow this two-year-long debate over strategic modernisation. But if the Commission on Strategic Forces was intended to be a fundamental reappraisal, it contained remarkably little reference to the prospect or merits of defence, as a concept, over deterrence. It is, however, of obvious interest in the search for the genesis of President Reagan's 'escape forward', represented by the ambition of the 'Star Wars' speech – strategic defence in space. The Chairman of the President's Commission on Strategic Forces (who gave his name to what was soon called the 'Scowcroft Commission') had been Henry Kissinger's deputy on the National Security Council staff, President Gerald Ford's special assistant for NSC affairs, and a member of President Carter's general advisory committee on arms control – General Brent Scowcroft.

GENERAL BRENT SCOWCROFT: We focused on three broad areas, with one major theme – which was the contribution to be made, in force structure, force development, and in arms control, to the enhancement of strategic stability between the two sides. So that, if you will, the character of the weapons systems in a crisis would not be an incentive to turn a crisis into a conflict. We thought there were three elements for that. The first was the MX which, we felt, was important both in redressing the imbalance in highly accurate missile warheads for deterrent purposes, and also as an incentive to move in other directions. Therefore the small *single*-warhead missile should be the direction in which ICBM forces should go: 'smallness' so that it could be mobile, and based in a variety of places which would increase its ability to survive; 'single-warhead' so as to reduce the value of the target, so that there was not this vast incentive to be able to destroy three, six, ten warheads with a single one. And the last was to integrate weapons procurement and development with arms control, in the direction of stability. In arms control, for example, to move toward 'de-MIRVing', toward reducing the value of each individual target.

CHARLTON: How did you mean to settle the anxieties which stalked the seminars and debates of the 1970s and which played such a strong role in the outcome of the 1980 election – this question of the vulnerability of America's land-based missiles and whether, by their very nature, arms control agreements had taken too little account of that vulnerability. Why did you validate the view, in the Scowcroft Commission, that vulnerability of this *particular force* by itself was relatively insignificant?

SCOWCROFT: What we tried to do was to divide the vulnerability question into two parts. Up to this time we had tried to solve the whole thing with *one* weapons system, the way Minuteman III had dealt with the problem a decade earlier. We decided that, in the present strategic environment, it was no longer possible to do that.

For the longer term issue of 'survivability' we looked to the small missile.[1] But over the short term we felt that there were other things for which MX was particularly suited. In other words, it was a kind of transitional system, to correct the imbalance which increased accuracy had developed between the Soviet and US forces. Both had increased their accuracy, but it redounded more to the benefit of the Soviets because of the character of their ICBM force. And as we looked at the vulnerability of the MX *itself*, we decided, first of all, that there was a lot of difference between the technical accuracy of a *test* missile, on a test range, and the system accuracy of *operational* weapons, fired by *operational* crews who seldom, if ever, practised with those weapons or could practise firing in a way to constitute the comprehensive attack which would be necessary for success. And the Soviets would have to have grave doubts about their ability concerning the second, whatever the technical accuracy of the first. I would say that judgment, in a sense, was validated by the Korean airliner

[1] i.e Midgetman

shoot-down. The Soviets had enormous confusion and problems on their side in dealing with what, after all, was a very *simple* penetration of their landmass.

People say the Scowcroft Commission did away with the 'window of vulnerability'. We didn't. What we said was, you have to look at this with a certain amount of perspective; and one perspective is the ability to do in *fact* what *technically* the weapons can do, in other words, your operational confidence in being able to do it. And the second part, as we addressed this issue of vulnerability, was this: that for now and for some time into the future, the missile forces and the bomber forces lend survivability to each other. The Soviets cannot attack both of them simultaneously. They need different weapons to attack them. And until such time as the Russians develop a highly accurate submarine-launched missile, the two will lend survivability to one another. For these reasons, and for any circumstance other than an absolute surprise attack – a bolt from the blue – we thought that MX was adequately survivable over the next decade or so.

CHARLTON: How big a factor in the deliberations of the Commission was uncertainty over the value of arms control as it had been practised and pursued?

SCOWCROFT: Our last letter to the President dealt almost exclusively with arms control. What we said was that, in the United States and in Western Europe, by and large the expectation for arms control had been too high. It was not going to solve all the East-West problems. It was not going to end the threat of nuclear war or the terrible devastation a nuclear war could bring. It could be a very useful device, if used in connection with weapons development, to enhance the stability of the balance.

CHARLTON: The arms control 'community' is divided by important differences of emphasis. Part of it believes that the arms race itself, by definition, is harmful to the interests of the United States and a danger to United States security . . .

SCOWCROFT: Very much so. We disagreed with that. I think that side is probably epitomised by the Freeze movement in the US. The assumption of the Freeze movement – that we are as well off as we can get and that any change has to be for the worst – we emphatically rejected that notion.

CHARLTON: What view did you take of the trends in strategic thinking beyond the broad assumptions of MAD, 'mutual assured destruction'? By which I mean a more vivid and explicit willingness to fight a nuclear war as a means of shoring up the concept of deterrence?

SCOWCROFT: While we did not deal with 'MAD' as a subject in and of itself, by and large I think the Commission rejected the notion of MAD – not the notion of deterrence. MAD, after all, is a kind of targeting doctrine. If you believe, literally, in the 'assured destruction' part of deterrence, then things like 'accuracy' and so on lose all their meaning, of course. By the very nature of our report, we did reject that.

We felt that by and large our nuclear forces *should* have a military and not simply a political rationale. Now, if you want to call that 'war-fighting' . . . I don't like that term because it is pejorative. What it *is*, is to try and calculate what, in fact, produces *deterrence*. I think we broadly felt (I may be speaking for myself here rather than the Commission) that one had to constantly *re-evaluate* deterrence: that we tended, in the United States, to look at deterrence from an American perspective which was largely irrelevant. From a deterrent standpoint, all that matters is what the *Soviets* think. We find little indication – from what we see of the kinds of forces they build, of how they deploy them, and in the exercises that we see them run – that assured destruction, the MAD idea, is anything the Soviets take very seriously.

CHARLTON: Is there not a danger that American strategic policy is likely to end up as a mirror image of Soviet policy? That, if you believe that they have a superior political and military rationale for the nuclear age, you are being drawn, increasingly, to imitate it rather than stand upon your own?

SCOWCROFT: No. That is a very good question and it certainly is a danger. But I think if one is mindful of the point that what we are trying to do is procure forces for *deterrence*, and that the Soviets – whatever their view of history and the 'inevitable outcome' which 'history' promises – are very cautious and very conservative, then one does not necessarily have to produce 'mirror-imaging' in order to affect their calculations.

CHARLTON: How did the Commission take into account the increasing capability for 'decapitating' strikes? As technology advances and accuracies improve comes the ability and the attraction of depriving the rival power of its government, of its centres of command and control – thus 'decapitating' the country.

SCOWCROFT: Well, it is a very serious problem. And I think we felt broadly that that was one of the elements in which both sides should seek a greater degree of stability. We felt that from a practical standpoint, while militarily it is attractive, politically it is not. It removes the possibility of negotiating, or 'de-celerating', if you will, a nuclear exchange. But the issue of decapitation is a very, very serious problem.

CHARLTON: In all the long report of the Scowcroft Commission, there are only a few paragraphs devoted to the issue of defence against ballistic missiles. Would you also agree that those few paragraphs were of a qualified enthusiasm for ballistic missile defence?

SCOWCROFT: Oh yes, I certainly would – and, I think, for a very good reason. There is nothing 'holy' about the Anti-Ballistic Missile Treaty. In the judgment of the Commission it served a useful purpose . . .

CHARLTON: You put that in the past tense?

SCOWCROFT: . . . up to the present time. The reason I put it in the past tense is that if we can achieve more in the way of deterrence and stability by modifying, or changing, the ABM treaty, we should not shrink from doing so, for that reason. I think that was, basically, our position. But it was also one of scepticism in the sense of, you know, 'proceed carefully', because there are things about strategic defence that can be destabilising. And so one ought to look very carefully at the whole issue before one launches off in a particular direction.

CHARLTON: Do you think the language of the treaty speaks clearly to the present technical and strategic realities?

SCOWCROFT: I had always thought that it was a very skilfully drawn treaty. I see now some loopholes I had not seen before. Some are ambiguous. The whole use of the term 'development', for example. Some kinds of development are prohibited by the ABM treaty. But 'development' is a word of art; it means something specific in terms of the Pentagon weapons acquisition process, but it's a very broad kind of term. The ABM treaty does not deal with anti-satellite systems. So it is not quite so iron-clad as I had thought before the strategic defence debate began.

CHARLTON: Why is ballistic missile defence suddenly to the fore, having been an outcast since the strategic debates of the 1960s?

SCOWCROFT: First, there are some who have always thought the ABM treaty was a mistake, and that strategic defence should always have been accorded a place; that we made a mistake in casting it into the outer darkness. It never was in the Soviet Union. They continued research after 1972. We did not, by and large. Indeed, until the President made his speech, one of the things we worried about most was the possibility of a Soviet 'break-out' in ABM because of their extensive research.

CHARLTON: Did the Commissioners share this view?

SCOWCROFT: No, we did not. I wouldn't say we had a particular view on that. ABM 'break-out' is a very complicated strategic question. But that was accompanied, I think, by a growing sense of frustration – as in the case of the Peace Movement, for example – with the notion of deterrence as it had existed: with the health of the world, if you will, resting on the rationality of a very few people in a couple of capital cities. I think for the President himself, this was very much present in his mind. The notion that, maybe, we can put this whole relationship on a more stable basis – rather than the awfulness of the MAD kind of deterrence.

CHARLTON: The critical question, in almost everything that you have said, is 'Will this enhance stability?'

SCOWCROFT: Very much so.

CHARLTON: What conclusions did you reach?

SCOWCROFT: Well, the Administration argues that *any* kind of defence, however ineffective it may prove to be in combat, enhances uncertainty. The attacker has to calculate the existence of defences. That adds to uncertainty and therefore to deterrence. That is almost a truism. But, you know, you have to look at the costs involved. Are there any *other* ways you can add to deterrence that are less costly, less destabilising? It is those kind of calculations that have to be gone into very carefully.

CHARLTON: What did the Scowcroft Commission contribute to that?

SCOWCROFT: We did not. We simply urged caution.

CHARLTON: What are the implications of the SDI as a path of development for strategic doctrine?

SCOWCROFT: I think the questions of defence are going to be with us from now on, whether we like it or not. I can identify at least five different versions of a strategic defence! It depends heavily on what one is trying to accomplish and how one goes about it. And whatever you think about the Soviet position, it *is* a tactical position – because they have, traditionally, been much more interested in defence than has the United States. They have a massive air defence system. They have an operating ABM system around Moscow (into which they pour billions and billions of dollars), and they have a very active R&D. Their strategic defence budget (one has to guess) is probably higher than that of the SDI at the present time; and they have active programmes on directed energy systems. Very much so. Therefore, whatever their arguments *now* about weapons in space, they are interested in strategic defence. We're really at the threshold. What we need to try to do is explore, deeply and dispassionately if we can, what kind of contribution (to the goals you and I have outlined here) strategic defence may be able to make.

CHARLTON: I don't for an instant, of course, suggest that you should be, but were you to be strapped to a lie-detector at this moment, what would be your reaction to a decision, to a determination, to *deploy* a strategic defence against ballistic missiles?

SCOWCROFT: I cannot answer. I don't think we know nearly enough. I would be much more comfortable in saying 'yes' to a deployment of a system to protect ICBMs – because I consider that to be, almost certainly, stabilising. The question there is not whether it makes *sense* but whether that is the best way to add to the survivability of the ICBM system – as opposed to other methods like mobility or concealment. Those are things you can look at realistically and analyse. Much, much more difficult are the questions of *population* defence.

CHARLTON: So the Scowcroft Commission had no trouble with a ballistic missile defence, constrained by the ABM treaty, in order to protect, for example, the Minutemen silos . . .

SCOWCROFT: No, not at all. Even seeking modification of the treaty in order to provide an adequate defence of missile systems. Absolutely. We recommended a vigorous R&D programme along those lines.

CHARLTON: On the other hand, a *space-based* defence, something which might challenge the whole core of deterrence, is not something with which you agree?

SCOWCROFT: I am reluctant to say 'space-based', because I don't think it's nearly so important *where* the systems are, as what it is they are designed to *do*. I think it is the notion of a *comprehensive* defence – one that may appear to an opponent as jeopardising his ability to penetrate – that is potentially the most destabilising aspect.

CHARLTON: It would be provocative?

SCOWCROFT: Yes. In the sense that if either side lost its ability to penetrate the territory of the other, then its strategic forces would be useless.

IN THE HISTORY OF THE NUCLEAR AGE such a condition has usually been reckoned one of great danger. On the evidence of its Chairman, General Brent Scowcroft, President Reagan's Commission on Strategic Forces can hardly be understood to have sounded the advance for a leap into the unknown, with defence as opposed to deterrence, becoming central to American strategy. While General Scowcroft maintains that he 'can identify at least five different versions of a strategic defence', overall he sustains the point made to us by Robert McNamara, at the outset, that the ambition of protecting weapons is good, while protecting populations is bad – the essence of deterrence.

But today, getting on for fifteen years since it was called into existence, General Scowcroft advises there can be 'nothing holy about the Anti-Ballistic Missile Treaty' – the principal symbol of deterrence. He acknowledges those trends in nuclear development which were nominated by Dr Keyworth, for example, as eroding confidence in deterrence as a concept: among them 'decapitation', that nuclear prescription for the Hobbesian proposition that because the state of nature is a state of war and insecurity, men – in order to escape the evils of their condition – will surrender their individual rights and constitute a state under an absolute sovereignty. Whether sovereignty is willed (as in the case of democracy) or not, 'decapitation', theoretically swift and surgically precise, renders that sovereignty – the seat of government itself, of power and control – most vulnerable of all. To Scowcroft it 'remains a very, very serious problem'.

In other words, the Scowcroft Commission conceded accumulating concerns which the 'star warriors' such as Dr Keyworth (the President's Science Adviser) have made a point of departure; and which, given the President's benediction and very large funding, create the atmosphere in which the 'Star Wars' concept is now being energetically pursued.

GEORGE KEYWORTH: To me it is the way science is pursued. Enormous numbers of questions are asked – an enormous number of arguments and debates go on – among scientists, the same way that, years ago, we began to pursue the question whether the neutrino possessed a mass, one of the more fundamental questions of physics today. This is the way we scientists work. It may appear to be chaotic, but I think that order ensues rather rapidly; and I think we are beginning to see a real order arise out of the SDI programme. We're beginning to see some of the very promising technologies emerge to destroy a ballistic missile in its *boost phase* – that missing capability that we simply did not know how to approach fifteen years ago.

SCEPTICAL AND INFORMED CRITICS MAINTAIN that the SDI's task of rendering nuclear weapons 'impotent' and 'obsolete' is of a different order of difficulty from anything so far within human technological accomplishment. But a 'star warrior' like Dr Keyworth recalls the precedents for such apostasy. A renowned predecessor as Science Adviser, Dr Vannevar Bush, told President Truman in 1945 that the ballistic missile would never possess the reliability or the accuracy to make it a significant weapon. In the British case, Professor F. A. Lindemann (Lord Cherwell) told Churchill the same thing about Hitler's V2, and (according to Edward Teller) in 1935 the great Lord Rutherford threw out of his office for 'talking nonsense' a Hungarian scientist who tried to persuade him that the atomic nucleus and its fantastic energy had practical applications.

Teller himself points to the arguments which preceded development of the hydrogen bomb in America in the 1950s. It was opposed, partly on moral grounds, by Robert Oppenheimer and Hans Bethe (one of the opponents of 'Star Wars' now) because, it was hoped, American restraint would encourage the Soviet Union to follow suit. But the Russians had already begun to build it, as so soon was made clear. They detonated their first hydrogen bomb only six months after the Americans.

Today research in the area of strategic defence is part of the technological landscape. The informed American position is that the Russians have worked long and hard – and to an extent unknown in the West – to hedge against the offensive strategic missile. What, then, are the similarities and points of departure with that other revolutionary strategic development – the decision over the H-bomb in the 1950s – as seen by the man who played a central role in it over thirty years ago?

EDWARD TELLER: Let me first start with the contrast. My opponents at that time argued against the hydrogen bomb, using the emphatic statement that the hydrogen bomb was 'too terrible'. Today the opponents (in remarkably many cases the very same people, in spite of the long time span) now say that *defensive* weapons will make atomic war look 'less terrible' and therefore more probable! We almost seem to have changed sides. I can accuse them of inconsistency; they can accuse me of inconsistency; yet, from another point of view, both sides have been consistent. In both cases, the opposition said no new technology is possible. In both cases the proponents, including myself, said it was. In the present case, mostly on the basis of the work of younger colleagues, we assert – and I assert – that these new technologies *are* possible and hopeful. I am only seventy-seven years old, and I am young enough to change my mind.

CHARLTON: But would it not be true to say that while you and your supporters have won the battle for public opinion, with Reagan's twice-elected administration, you appear to have lost it with your fellow scientists?

TELLER: We have not won it yet with the ancient ones whose mental inertia seems to surpass the inertia of any other known substance. I haven't given up hope. They say a 'complete defence' is impossible. *Of course* it's impossible. War without risk, or peace without risk, or life without risk, is impossible. But to claim that defence is more risky than the balance of terror, with lots of terror and hardly any balance at all? That, I think that should sink in. I think the hope of deterring war by *defence* is our best hope. And in the very worst case – even though the consequence of war may be worse than anything we can remember, though perhaps not worse than anything recorded in history – defence might suffice to save some remnants of our civilisation. I have lived with the fear of an atomic war for a little longer than forty-six years, and I have never felt as hopeful as I feel now – because I see the light at the end of the tunnel. And I am no longer alone. Many of the young scientists are with us.

AND SO, THIRTY YEARS AFTER he became known as the father of the H-bomb, Dr Edward Teller issues the challenge of his own authority to the strategic axiom which the Bomb introduced – that the intrinsic superiority of defence cannot exist in our epoch. History suggests that where the prospect of military advantage exists, it is the Tellers of this world who will prevail. But there has been a considerable backing away from the more or less 'complete' defence envisaged by President Reagan in his 'Star Wars' speech – a shift which itself is almost a study in exegesis. After the speech, for some six months in 1983, the President ordered two studies of the concept of strategic defence: one to look into the technologies, the other to examine the policy implications in strategy (and arms control) for America and its allies. This second (for the most part still classified) study was conducted by a team of advisers led by Fred Hoffman.

FRED HOFFMAN: The President used very general terms in that speech; and some of them clearly have to be viewed as Presidential rhetoric. I remember I worked for a President once when I was in the government, and in a speech he said he was going to eliminate poverty.

CHARLTON: Lyndon Johnson?

HOFFMAN: That was Lyndon Johnson, right. Nevertheless, President Reagan used one phrase that I think is worth remembering, because it illustrates my view more or less precisely. He said he wanted to make nuclear weapons 'impotent' and 'obsolete'. I think it is worth reflecting on the difference between those two terms. In my view it is possible to work toward defences that may make ballistic missiles at least obsolete, and to have a prospect of getting to that conclusion long before the advance of defensive technology will be able to make nuclear weapons *impotent* (if indeed they ever can). The difference, I think, lies in the fact that for something to become *obsolete*, it doesn't need to be *impotent*. The crossbow is not impotent, yet it is obsolete as a weapon. It has been superseded because it is no longer militarily useful.

CHARLTON: But I'd like to quote to you what you said in the Hoffman Report on the SDI. When you say 'partial systems, or systems with more modest technical goals, may be more feasible earlier than the full system . . .', we should be in no doubt, should we, that you're walking away from the President's dream?

HOFFMAN: Yes and no. We, in our dreams, may dream that we can fly and it's a pleasant sensation. Similarly, it would be very pleasant – and a better world in my view – if we *could* become invulnerable to nuclear weapons. On the other hand, I do not believe that I'm walking away from the President's objective of enhancing deterrence, of getting a better and more suitable basis for deterrence, and of protecting people, protecting civilians. There the key assumption is about the kind of attack that you believe it is necessary to protect against.

If you believe that the only defences worth having are those that will work against an attack in which the Soviet Union devotes the bulk of its forces to attacking *cities*, then indeed you need almost perfect defences in order to achieve a reasonable level of that objective. If you think you're concerned about an attack in which the primary objective of the Soviet Union is to attack *military targets* (but in which they may, if they do it, inflict very large collateral damage), then I believe that much more moderate levels of defence capability can both deter the attack *and protect the civilians* against the collateral damage, if the attack occurs.

One of the implications of ballistic missile defence may be that it makes obsolete the notion of massive nuclear attacks, in order to lay waste a country. That is to say, it raises the question of *selective* attacks as the only nuclear option that may make sense. My own view, and this depends on the outcome of some technical questions, is that the way in which ballistic missile defences will be beaten – to the extent to which they may be beaten, and if they are beaten – will not be through 'mass', through saturating them. I think that, given likely attack objectives, it will turn out to be prohibitive to simply try to saturate ballistic missile defences. I think that if they're to be beaten, they'll have to be beaten qualitatively.

CHARLTON: My recollection is that that's not what you said, however, in the Hoffman Report. You thought that the Soviet response was likely to be their traditional one – that they would augment their offensive forces.

HOFFMAN: Their *initial* response – depending on their judgment of the technology. Now, I am not at all sure that we *will* see that response, or that it will be manifest. I think that when faced with the possible deployment of ballistic missile defences, they – and we – will both know more about the character of those defences than we do now. My own view is that the likely character of those defences, at the time we think we might deploy them, is going to be such that it will be relatively unattractive to simply force one's way through by brute force. I think the implication of that is that the game is going to go to the side that is more *clever*; and the feasible kinds of attack objectives are going to look increasingly limited and selective.

THE PROPONENTS OF SDI BELIEVE that, in the long run, Fred Hoffman's analysis mitigates or disposes of Robert McNamara's contention to the Russians in the 1960s (which became the basis of the Anti-Ballistic Missile Treaty): that to attempt 'defence' would lead only to more and more strategic missiles to overwhelm that defence. Today, the 'star warriors' see the Strategic Defence Initiative as both the means and the incentive to compel those reductions in offensive missiles which were supposed to follow in the wake of the ABM treaty, more than a decade ago, and which arms control has not been able to achieve.

But McNamara's more fundamental point was the futility of the pursuit of advantage in the age of the absolute weapon. And this is the challenge of 'Star Wars'. While the President's vision of 'defending populations' has not been disavowed, Fred Hoffman makes obvious the incompatibilities between the near and long-term issues posed by strategic defence. In the beginning, by defence of weapons and military installations (it is argued), it will enhance nuclear deterrence. But in the end, comprehensive space-based defences, if successful in defending populations, will eliminate the need for deterrence. Concerning nuclear deterrence, can the SDI have it both ways? Thucydides, the historian of the Peloponnesian War who 'set down nothing but facts', decided that what made war inevitable was the growth of Athenian power and the fear this caused in Sparta. President Nixon, we might recall, on taking office and arguing for the ABM treaty, echoed that ancient concern:

> While I would like to provide the American people with complete protection against nuclear attack, it is not now within our power to do so. It might look to an opponent like the prelude to an offensive strategy threatening the Soviet deterrent.

How is the transition from the present reality to the President's vision to take place? The voices which, in terms of direct influence, bestride the American strategic debate today speak differently to this issue than their counterparts in the 1960s. Among the most influential of them on American attitudes to arms control and nuclear weapons has been Senator Henry Jackson's former aide (who drafted much of the Senator's early opposition to the SALT agreements). Richard Perle is now Assistant Secretary of Defence. Should both the United States and the Soviet Union move towards strategic defence?

RICHARD PERLE: I believe *the United States* should move to a strategic defence. The situation is a little bit different for the Soviet Union whose offensive forces, whose technology and technology base, strategic doctrine and objectives are all, in my view, quite different. But I think it is most unwise for us to compete with the Soviet Union in an area where they have considerable advantages. With respect to the continuing production of offensive forces, in particular land-based ballistic missiles, the Soviets have enormous advantages. They can move missiles freely about the country, the landmass over which they can move them is many times larger than the United States. They don't have to worry about safety and security with respect to terrorists (as we do), and so it is easy and relatively efficient for them to go on adding offensive nuclear missiles to their inventory. It's far more difficult for us to do that. We by contrast have, I believe, long-term technological advantages, based not on the current state of our knowledge about strategic defence (because we are behind the Soviet Union today), but because we have a much richer technological base on which to draw. It makes sense, in my view, to compete with the Soviets where we are strongest, on *our* playing-field, and not where we are weakest, on *theirs*.

CHARLTON: The historical precedent for treating the SDI as a bargaining counter, as leverage, is already established (some would say) with the 1972 agreement, the history of ABM defence and the treaty. Are you saying that the SDI programme should be protected? Or should we see it as another go round the same circuit as in 1972, where the sacrifice of this no doubt very substantial pawn would produce a new equilibrium and a new hope?

PERLE: You've put the question in a provocative way, because it seems to suggest that far from *learning* from the experience of 1972, we will simply repeat it. In 1972 the American ABM system was one that we were capable of deploying. It was regarded as a 'bargaining chip' because it was believed that we could obtain from the Soviet Union limitations on their offensive forces that would obviate the requirement for an American defence. Two things have happened since. One is that the Soviet forces grew beyond even our most pessimistic expectations under the terms of the 1972 agreement. So the objective of obviating the requirement for a defence was not reached. Secondly, to add insult to injury, the Soviets recognised in 1972 that they were behind the United States in defensive technology and they greatly increased their investment in defensive technology. The result is that today they are in a position to deploy an anti-ballistic missile defence of roughly the same technology that we were looking at in 1972 – and we are not. There is very considerable evidence that the Soviets may be doing precisely that. The construction of a network of radars (the most recent of which, at Krasnoyarsk, is a clear violation of the ABM treaty), together with a vigorous programme modernising the Moscow ABM system, and the development of air-defence missiles that also have a capability in combination with it – all points in the direction of the Soviets acquiring a capacity to strike American ballistic missiles.

CHARLTON: On the specific point of the new radar at Krasnoyarsk, the Soviet Union claims that this *is* within the limits of the ABM agreement as it interprets it. Are we back to the old question of 'intentions' and 'capabilities'? Or is this new radar susceptible of only one intention and therefore no other explanation?

PERLE: I think it is the latter. I think the Soviets are lying when they attribute a different function to it. I think that they sat down in Moscow; they concluded that there was a gap in the comprehensive radar coverage of the Soviet Union which, if permitted to continue, would make the deployment of a nationwide defence impossible. They decided to proceed with it and they decided they would call it something else if they were challenged.

The Soviets claim it is a space-tracking radar. Space-tracking radars, as you might imagine, are oriented toward *space*, which is where the objects to be tracked are found. The radar at Krasnoyarsk is *not* oriented toward space but toward the *horizon*, where one finds very few objects in orbit – but where one does indeed find ballistic missiles on their trajectories toward targets in the Soviet Union. Moreover, the radar at Krasnoyarsk is identical with other radars in the Soviet Union (including one at Pechora) that, prior to our discovery of the radar at Krasnoyarsk, they acknowledged as being early-warning radars – which is precisely what one would put at Krasnoyarsk as part of the infrastructure for an ABM system. Space-tracking radars are relatively cheap to build. The Soviets already possess them. When you build one, you don't surround it with thousands of tons of concrete unless you expect it to come under attack (as one must expect with an anti-ballistic missile defence radar) – in which case you build it exactly as they have built the radar at Krasnoyatsk.

CHARLTON: If you lived in Europe and you studied the weapons being built by the United States, rather than the publicly articulated policy of the United States, why should the Europeans not see strategic defence as making possible a degree of American detachment or disengagement – an option the United States has not had since more or less the end of World War II?

PERLE: I think it's really quite the reverse. The fundamental point about the American involvement in Europe, in a security sense, is the commitment of the United States to come to the defence of Europe, symbolised by the presence of over 200,000 American troops in Europe, and the commitment to use nuclear weapons, if necessary, for the defence of Europe. As you well know, there have been doubts expressed with varying degrees of candour, from the earliest days of that commitment, whether the United States *would*, in a crisis, honour the commitment to use nuclear weapons for Europe's defence. *With* a defence, with the United States *protected* from attack – I think doubts about the willingness to meet that commitment would vanish.

CHARLTON: Why does not strategic defence mitigate 'flexible response' when it weakens the authority of nuclear weapons – on which deterrence relies?

PERLE: The principal problem with the doctrine of 'flexible response' is whether it is credible at the nuclear level. The essence of flexible response is that the Alliance is prepared to respond, at whatever level it takes, to protect the Alliance. When you get to the nuclear level there are serious questions about the credibility of the American nuclear commitment. So I think that a *defended* America is more likely to be understood by the Soviet Union to *mean* it when it says it will defend Europe with nuclear weapons. So I think it strengthens flexible response.

The SDI is often described as an effort to erect a dome over the United States, with Soviet Union missiles bouncing off that dome. In fact, the thrust of the American strategic defence programme is aimed at technologies that would intercept Soviet missiles while they are still over Soviet territory. A better way to look at it is that we are attempting to put a dome over the *Soviet Union* that will keep Soviet missiles *in*. In that image, the relationship between Europe and the United States and Europe and the Soviet Union is quite different.

One can take the view that if the United States proceeds with strategic defence, the Soviets will inevitably follow suit. That carries with it the implication that if the United States forbears, the Soviet Union will also forbear. I don't believe that for a moment. I think the Soviets will proceed with strategic defence, if they're capable of doing so, independent of what the United States does. They started research on lasers, and particle beams, and directed energy devices long before we did. They're marching down that path. They would prefer to march down that path alone (and hence their current effort to dissuade the United States from continuing). But there isn't any doubt in my mind that they will pursue research on defensive technologies – and, if successful, deploy them – whether we do or not.

RICHARD PERLE'S OPINION that the Americans should compete with the Soviet Union on the ground where they, the Americans, are strongest, conforms to the analysis made more than a century ago by Alexis de Tocqueville of the then emerging two great powers. Tocqueville saw their struggle as one between 'dominion over nature' and 'dominion over people'. The American, he said, struggles against the obstacles of nature; the adversaries of the Russian are men. The former combats the wilderness, the latter civilisation. The principle of the American is 'freedom', of the Russian 'servitude'. Ever since World War II, the West has sought to defend itself by technological superiority rather than the huge conventional array of force at the disposal of a permanently mobilised society such as the Soviet Union. The energies driving the American ambition for strategic defence lie in the path of that history. Whether the President's SDI is negotiable with the Russians in return for the 'restraint' and for the 'deep cuts' in missiles they refused President Carter – President Reagan says it is not negotiable – whether it will, in the end, be the impulse which allows Sisyphus to push the arms control boulder up the hill once more, has brought us to the current controversy, which will dominate debate and summit meetings in the years to come.

In the first chapter of this 'Star Wars' history, Gerard Smith (head of the American delegation to the 1972 SALT talks which resulted in the Anti-Ballistic Missile Treaty) recalled for us his impression that an audible 'sigh of relief' came from Britain and from France when they saw the signatures fixed to that treaty. Limiting ballistic missile defences (around Moscow) made valid the 'independent deterrent threat' of the smaller British and French nuclear forces. It was part of the remit given by President Reagan to Fred Hoffman's team of experts that they also examine the consequences of 'Star Wars' for the deterrents of the smaller nuclear powers.

FRED HOFFMAN: It was clear that questions were going to arise about the implications of SDI for national nuclear forces, and they have indeed arisen. Questions would also arise with regard to the viability of the strategy of 'selective response' – selective 'offensive' response, in the presence of defences. However, both these issues involve an implicit assumption, and I think it is absolutely crucial. The assumption is that if the United States abstains from the pursuit of ballistic missile defences, the Soviets will also abstain indefinitely. Because it is clearly not the American defences that threaten the national nuclear forces, or that threaten the policy of selective response. It is the Soviet defences that do that.

CHARLTON: What conclusion did you come to about the implications of the SDI for the small deterrent forces?

HOFFMAN: I think the SDI doesn't have any very direct implications for the small nuclear forces. It may at the margin: that is to say, the results of the SDI might move a Soviet decision to deploy ballistic missile defences forward, or backward, some years in time. But, in my view, if there exists in nature a relatively effective set of technologies for ballistic missile defences waiting to be discovered, the Soviets will discover them sooner or later, *and they will deploy them.*

It seems to me that it's possible to argue the effect of SDI, on that particular front, in either direction. If you believe that, in the absence of any significant effort by the United States, the Soviets might have greater incentives to abrogate the ABM treaty at some point than they otherwise would, then in effect SDI (by providing deterrence to such an abrogation) would presumably assist in maintaining the effectiveness of smaller nuclear forces. If it has the reverse effect, if it leads the Soviets to believe that they have nothing to lose, then it would precipitate the problem sooner than it otherwise would occur. But either way, it seems to me that the basic issue – as long as the United Kingdom and France maintain the national decision to keep national nuclear forces – is one of co-operation with regard to the objectives of those forces and the technical support of those forces. And there, one of the functions of SDI will be to give a better understanding of what it will take to attempt to penetrate ballistic missile defences. In that regard there is an avenue for co-operation, if it's judged to be in the national interest.

CHARLTON: But would you agree that, historically, American thinking about this has not always been consistent? There has been support for the 'second centre of decision' in the Nixon Administration; not much before that, Robert McNamara (as in his Athens speech) in the 1960s was quite opposed to it.

HOFFMAN: I must confess to not being an enthusiast for national nuclear forces.

CHARLTON: Because it complicates the American position?

HOFFMAN: It complicates the American position and it diverts resources from what we believe were higher Alliance uses.

CHARLTON: But did you come to different conclusions in the 1980s than were reached, for example, at Nassau, between Macmillan and Kennedy in the 1960s, where the British (and subsequently the French) proved that a national nuclear deterrent was something they were absolutely unwilling to surrender?

HOFFMAN: Kennedy accepted it, and I believe the United States can do little else but accept it so long as this is the national position of the countries involved. I think that the questions of what the mutual interests of the United States and the European countries involved are – and what the implications are for co-operation – are ones that do need to be exercised *now* within the context of the Strategic Defence Initiative.

BOTH GREAT POWERS ARE SET on a path of research and development which could carry them beyond the strategic capabilities of the individual nation states of Western Europe, Britain and France, who have determined to maintain themselves as nuclear powers. Should that situation arise it would be unique in the nuclear age. The open-ended possibilities of strategic defence are therefore of obvious European interest and of special concern to Britain and to France.

★ 6 ★
EUROPE AND AMERICA:

Reconciled among the Stars?

PRESIDENT REAGAN'S INSTALLING of strategic defence as a new and active American ambition has widened the range of possibilities and uncertainties which surround Western Europe. The evidence so far suggests that it has presented the Soviet Union with a thought-provoking, even compelling challenge. It has also concentrated the minds of America's allies, whose responses have seemed to be divided between fascination and fright. Officially, as Churchill once remarked in another context, they have appeared to find 'little difficulty in restraining their enthusiasm within the bounds of decorum'.

Among the arguments put forward in support of 'Star Wars' has been that it is unreasonable to suppose that any system of security, including nuclear deterrence, can function at all times and endure for decade after decade. The remark from another epoch, of England's 'gloomy dean', Dean Inge, concerning the Gadarene swine – 'No doubt they felt the going was good for the first half of the way' – is reflected in President Reagan's persuasion that the threat of mutual annihilation is at once morally wrong and increasingly unstable. No doubt, either, that critics of the SDI maintain their belief that deterrence has worked for forty years or more and 'if it ain't broke, why fix it?'.

The announced intention of 'Star Wars' is to substitute 'assured survival' for the present nuclear reality of 'assured destruction' based upon the threat of retaliation in kind. Where then do the principal European concerns arise? We must turn to European political leaders who have dealt with strategic nuclear choices in the past. The eventual goal of the 'Star Wars' initiative is to create defences so strong that there can be no assurance that ballistic missiles can overwhelm them. Ever since the first Soviet intercontinental rocket put an end to the privileged immunity of the homelands of the United States, America has shared the risks of nuclear war with its allies in Western Europe. Inevitably, 'strategic defence' raises doubts about the equality of that shared risk in the future. And if the Soviet Union were to follow suit and make a success of its own active research and development of a 'Star Wars' defence, it would mean a Russia freed from the deterrent threat of nuclear reprisal and, it's argued, a Europe made safer for war – whether nuclear or conventional.

President Reagan's vision of an America shielded comprehensively against nuclear ballistic missiles, by layers of defences on earth and in space, departs fundamentally from the expressed principal purpose of the Anti-Ballistic Missile Treaty of 1972 which, with the Americans opting for MAD, all but abandoned the idea of strategic defence. The 1972 treaty took account of the already existing Soviet ABM defences around Moscow (concerning which, as he has told us earlier, Robert McNamara had his heated exchanges with the Soviet Prime Minister Kosygin during the Johnson Presidency). Since the 1960s, exercising an option under the treaty which the Americans did not take up for Washington, the Russians have been the only ones to deploy, and they have constantly modernised, around the Soviet capital, a treaty-limited system of ballistic missile defences.

The British nuclear deterrent, on twenty-four-hour patrol beneath the oceans, is directly linked in a causal relationship to the *limited* defences which the ABM treaty permits. As the Russians have updated the ABM defence of Moscow, the British in reply have made the costly improvement of the Chevaline warhead to the Polaris missiles of the Royal Navy's submarines to assure the threat of British retaliation in the face of those (still limited) defences. For a small deterrent force (although of very great destructive power), Chevaline *and* the ABM treaty were both judged necessary to make the British deterrent credible (otherwise to be seen as, increasingly, a national eccentricity). That was the thrust of the advice given to successive British governments by the Chief Scientific Adviser of the time, Professor Sir Hermann Bondi.

SIR HERMANN BONDI: The system the Russians deployed was one that worked outside the atmosphere, and which sought to injure incoming warheads which originally had been designed without this thought occurring in one's mind, and were therefore exceedingly vulnerable. The British deterrent, as it existed until a few years ago, would not have been able to count on getting through to the Moscow area. Until the Anti-Ballistic Missile Treaty came along there was, of course, no reason to expect that the Soviet Union would not deploy similar defences around most of the other Soviet cities. This was later restricted by the ABM treaty, and further restricted by the Protocol. The treaty meant that only one city was defended. The advice clearly had to be that if our force was targeted on Moscow, it was quite likely – not certain, but quite likely – to be ineffective.

CHARLTON: So the bearing that the Soviet defence – the modernisation of the Russian ballistic missile defence system around Moscow – has had on the modernisation of our own nuclear deterrent is clear. There is a direct link?

BONDI: There is, of course – on the basis of the political attitude to what one might call 'the Moscow criterion'.

CHARLTON: Can you say why it is that the British have dedicated the nuclear deterrent to the city of Moscow, the so-called 'Moscow criterion'?

BONDI: The whole aim of deterrence is to keep the peace and, within that peace, to keep the Western Alliance inviolate. Now, within this Alliance, quite clearly some members are more directly under Soviet pressure, or the possibility of that pressure, than others. From the whole point of view of a British deterrent – from the whole point of view of a second centre of decision within the Alliance – the impression this makes on our *friends* and *allies* is at least as important as what our putative enemies think of it. For us to resign ourselves to have a capability that is not only quantitatively small but *qualitatively* second-rate would severely diminish the political effect, within the Alliance, of having a deterrent at all. So 'the Moscow criterion' goes rather far. It's rather important in the context of Alliance politics.

As far as 'the other side' is concerned, one is of course talking of a highly centralised system, centralised in a manner we can hardly imagine. No doubt they will take precautions. They *have* taken certain precautions – but the enormous importance of Moscow in the Soviet Union is quite clear. So abandoning 'the Moscow criterion' would be a very severe reduction in what one might call 'the quality of the deterrent' and its prime task of helping to keep the peace.

CHARLTON: The historical evidence, would you agree, is that the Soviet Union has managed to follow, and to cover, technological advances by the United States. What are the implications of strategic defence, as you see them, for the *small* deterrent force – be it British, French or Chinese?

BONDI: I think this is a very involved question because it rests, or relates, to a number of different points. For a small country like the United Kingdom (even France is a fairly small country from this point of view), I think you have to wonder at every stage whether your deterrent increases, or decreases, your security. It is quite clear that if *all* you had was a first-strike weapon, vulnerable to a counterstroke, then that would be diminishing rather than increasing your security. The only way to *increase* one's security is to rely totally on a *second-strike* weapon – one that can survive an attack. The only way we can ensure that is by hiding our weapon under the ocean.

So I would like to put your question in this form: will the oceans remain opaque? Enormous amounts of brain power and money have been poured into making the oceans *transparent*. My feeling is that the submarine designers have been rather more successful than the 'ocean-penetrating-glance' people; so, for the time being, the ocean is a marvellous hiding place. In relation to the Strategic Defence Initiative, whether it would work against not a *long-range* intercontinental missile but a short-range one, fired from a submarine, is a matter to be investigated. If submarines stay secure I think we are in a relatively good position.

But it is worth talking at this moment about an essential asymmetry between the two superpowers, which is something that gives me considerable concern. It is that, if the ocean remains opaque, targets on or near the shore will remain at risk against almost any technical advance. Not quite every – but almost any. The Western Alliance is full of targets *close to the shore*. The Soviet Union does not have that at all, at least as long as we feel that the Baltic cannot easily be penetrated. So a situation in which the only successful use of strategic nuclear weapons could be relatively *short-range* from the ocean, against a coastal target, would put the Western Alliance at a tremendous disadvantage. I find *that* a worrying aspect of this evolution.

EUROPEAN GOVERNMENTS HAVE BEEN particularly reluctant to forsake historical positions linking security with national sovereignty, but, as Sir Hermann Bondi makes apparent, the prospect of 'Star Wars' defences has implications for both. For almost half a century, since the feasibility of the atomic bomb was demonstrated, Britain has been involved in making nuclear weapons and has shown itself, under all post-war British governments, determined to do what was necessary to maintain for the last resort an independent nuclear deterrent. But it has not been consistent American policy that Britain should be assisted to do so. The history of what became the 'interdependent nuclear relationship' with the United States is marked by episodes which amounted almost to the unilateral nuclear disarmament of Britain by her closest ally – and which had a seismic effect on the Anglo-American political relationship.

Since that time Britain has taken a number of steps which emphasise her relationship with Europe, above all her membership of the European Community. In history's broader sweep, it is possible to see that Britain has been slowly grafted back on to the body politic of Europe since the Entente Cordiale and before World War I. It was the humiliation of the British and French intervention in Suez in 1956 – which forced the realisation that the United Kingdom alone could no longer conduct a sovereign military and political policy in any part of the world against American opposition – which provided what was perhaps the most powerful impulse for Britain to reconsider her early post-World War II attitudes to Europe and, eventually, to seek membership of the Community.

How is the issue presented by a possible move to strategic defence judged today – alongside those other strategic nuclear issues which arose in the past – by the Prime Minister who took Britain into Europe, Edward Heath. (He had also been Chief Whip in Anthony Eden's Conservative

Government at the time of Suez.) Edward Heath's own administration, in 1970, took the decision to modernise the British nuclear deterrent.

EDWARD HEATH: I suppose the first similarity one looks to is the joint work which was done during the Second World War on atomic developments, and then what Congress did directly after the War. Through the MacMahon Act, Congress said that none of the information is to be available to the other powers who have taken part in this joint work. I think we ought to remember that lesson; it's a very hard lesson to learn.

When you come to the question of the SDI, then a lot of new questions are raised. The first is, can any system be absolutely fool-proof, either from the human or the 'hardware' point of view? Can we ever rely on this entirely as a defensive mechanism, in space, to prevent us being attacked by nuclear weapons? I do not believe that it's possible for any system to be completely fool-proof. You have human weaknesses, and we constantly see weaknesses in the 'hardware'. Well then, you can't rely on the SDI alone, which means you still must have the deterrent force. Any substitute for the deterrent is just not enough. This, I think, is the first thing one has to realise about the SDI.

Then come the questions. If that is *not* enough, should we be spending a vast amount of money on research and development in order to get such a system? Ought we not also to recognise that the American military machine is so powerful that it won't stop at 'Research and Development'? It'll be bound to lead to deployment – and that means spending many more millions. This, of course, is then an armaments race. The Soviet Union is bound to follow. There will be no question of it staying behind. An arms race is not in the interest of either the East or the West. We should do everything possible in order to stop that.

Looking at it from our own point of view, certain questions repeat themselves. If we take part in the Strategic Defence Initiative research and development, it means using a considerable part of our resources. What are we going to get out of it at the end? To all intents and purposes, nothing. The Americans will keep control of any system which does come out of it. US commerce and US firms will keep control of any commercial advantages, and we in Europe shall get nothing. The deduction from that is one which I have made before, and that is that Europe must be looking after its own affairs in *conjunction* with an Alliance, but not *subservient* to it. That was, after all, the point of the British keeping their nuclear deterrent, and the reason why the French developed theirs. I proposed long ago (in 1967, I think it was) in my Godkin Lectures at Harvard, that the British and the French deterrent should be joined together. You could do it in a variety of ways, and I suggested one or two, but that has unfortunately never come about. But that is what I would like to have seen, and would still like to see today.

CHARLTON: Scientific performance and achievement have been insepar-able from the Anglo-American special relationship. But would you agree that that is a gap which, over the years, has got wider and wider between the United Kingdom and the United States – and it was a gap which was first obvious in this atomic field? There's been Polaris; Trident has a question mark against it because of its great cost; and SDI is quite beyond us as a nation state. What questions do you feel that raises?

EDWARD HEATH: Of course the first instance which one goes back to is Skybolt[1], which had been promised to us by the United States but which was then discarded by President Kennedy. They really proposed to put nothing in its place, which would have left us without any defence at all in the nuclear field. It was only after very long arguments between Harold Macmillan and President Kennedy (and I think the Prime Minister's personal influence, really, with the President decided that) that it was agreed we would in fact get the Polaris. Now that was under certain very rigid conditions, but we did maintain the position that in the event of our deciding it was our own national emergency, then we would have the use of it. So the present situation does lead back to that question: ought we not to develop our own resources so that we are not entirely dependent in that way on the decision, not necessarily of the *Administration*, but of the *Congress*?

CHARLTON: It's been said that there is no cost to the United States in the special relationship. What do you think the cost of the special relationship is to the United Kingdom?

EDWARD HEATH: It can be high if we do things just for the sake of pleasing the United States or a Prime Minister pleasing a President. That, in my view, is not a proper consideration of national interest. I've always said that what we have between Britain and America is a *natural* relationship. All sorts of people can have 'special relationships'. The Germans can have a special relationship because of their economic strength. What we have is a natural relationship founded on the relationships of many families both sides of the Atlantic, on what was a common language and a common legal system. That is something nobody can ever destroy. We have to use that natural relationship to the best advantage of both sides of the Atlantic; and we do that by the place we have in Europe.

The national interest is to look after our own position in Europe, which is our own continent and in which we have our economic future as a member of the European Community. I believe that this will have to extend to include defence to a far greater extent than it does at the moment. Otherwise, we shall just lose the technology. Unless we reorganise our procurement for defence requirements as a Community,

---

[1] an American air-launched missile designed to be carried by the Royal Air Force V-bombers and with a British nuclear warhead

we will lose our knowledge, we will lose our young people – who will go
off to other cities and other countries where they can find it.

CHARLTON: Do you feel that the SDI, or the issues posed by the SDI, have
particular relevance to that?

EDWARD HEATH: Yes, I think it has. Let us look at our national interest
very clearly. Is it in our national interest for a large amount of money to be
poured into research and development of SDI in order to please the
Americans – or so that the Americans can say to the Soviet Union, 'Well, it
isn't just *us*, it's the whole of Europe . . .'? No. I don't believe it is.

IN THE THIRTY YEARS SINCE the Messina Conference of 1955 founded the
European Community, the states of Western Europe have had the time to
pursue joint foreign, security and defence policies. They have made small
headway. Edward Heath's advocacy of a special relationship with the
Community – to complement what he considered to be the natural
relationship with the United States – is a step over which his successors
have shown themselves to be more hesitant.

Back in 1962, when Skybolt was cancelled, it was seen by Harold
Macmillan and his ministers as an American attempt to contrive, as a
corollary of cancellation, the end of the independent British nuclear
deterrent. It was US policy to encourage integration of the British and
French deterrents in a multinational force within NATO and under US
control. That this is still a theme, at least, in American considerations, was
apparent from Fred Hoffman (who led one of President Reagan's teams of
advisers on the consequences of 'Star Wars' for Alliance politics) when he
said, 'I must confess to not being an enthusiast for national nuclear forces
. . . they complicate the American position and divert resources from what
we believe to be higher Alliance purposes.'

In its possible effects, if not its intention, the 'Star Wars' concept invites
comparison with questions raised in the dispute over the multinational
force in the 1960s. When Harold Macmillan, rather than explore nuclear
collaboration with France, persuaded President Kennedy to give Britain
the Polaris submarine (and to offer the same arrangements to the French),
General de Gaulle considered that the British Prime Minister's choice
dramatised a fundamental difference between them about the future of
Europe. He vetoed Britain's first attempt to join the European Community, and it is also a reason why there are two national nuclear forces in
Europe today. The SDI and its Soviet counterpart give warning of the
possible obsolescence of the independent nuclear deterrents of Britain and
France, and thus mitigate their deterrent threat. How, this time, might
Britain and France face a prospect created by the SDI (IDS to the French)
which they last confronted in 1962?

General de Gaulle's legacy is symbolised by the wholly independent
nuclear deterrent of France – those supreme instruments of national power
to which de Gaulle himself attached such prestige and importance – and

the disbelief that the United States would commit nuclear suicide for its allies in Europe. In terms of history, therefore, how does the new American initiative compare with the way the 'nuclear choices' have declared themselves in the past? Maurice Couve de Murville was General de Gaulle's Foreign Minister and is still a guardian of the General's pervasive 'Gaullist' legacy.

MAURICE COUVE DE MURVILLE: The first thing to say is that it is difficult to know exactly what it's all about. I think nobody has the answer now, even the people in the United States who are busy with this new system. It seems to me that, in principle, the case of the United States is very different from the case of my country, France, because this IDS system seems to be oriented towards defence against *strategic* nuclear weapons and not *tactical* nuclear weapons; that is, against weapons coming to the United States from the Soviet Union and not on weapons coming from the Soviet Union in the direction of Western Europe. In other words, it is a system not at the present directly concerning West European countries, but the security – and therefore the strategy – of the United States.

In principle, we could believe now that, if this IDS comes to work in the Soviet Union after the United States, it will be a defence against the strategic weapons that the British and French have built and that are directed against the Soviet Union. In other words, our nuclear submarines. It is possible, and (believing what we are being told now) it is even probable, that we should have to review the system – in order to have a nuclear deterrent capable of continuing to be a threat to the Soviet Union, in spite of the new defences that the Soviet Union is going to build.

CHARLTON: Given the enormous cost of nuclear deterrence and now, as one must presume, space-based defences, are these both within the reach of France, do you suppose?

COUVE DE MURVILLE: It is, of course, hard to answer the question now. Forty years ago, when the nuclear armament system began to develop (in the United States, of course), everybody thought that it was such a secret – and such a financial burden – that only the United States would be capable in the future of doing that. Maybe one day, we thought, the Soviet Union could; but certainly far behind the United States. Now, forty years afterwards, we have a situation where the fabrication of nuclear weapons is no longer a secret. Everybody knows. And it is not such a financial burden either. Britain, France and China – and probably, secretly, others like Israel and South Africa – have been capable of building these weapons without destroying their financial equilibrium.

Will the evolution of things be the same with this IDS business? Nobody can say. Maybe in ten or twenty years, the secrets of 'Star Wars' will no longer be a secret. It is possible. Now there is something, of course, we can imagine – apart from Britain or France building a system of its own. We can imagine a sort of co-operation between European countries; as long as this was not a system for waging war but a *defence* system, a system not to strike the Soviet Union but to defend ourselves against Soviet weapons.

CHARLTON: Do you think a 'European' defence role is conceivable and useful?

COUVE DE MURVILLE: If you mean by that an organisation between the main countries of Western Europe, to be capable of defending itself against the Soviet Union, that is not very likely – for two reasons. One reason is that you have in Western Europe only two nuclear countries. The third big country, Germany, will never be allowed to have nuclear weapons. The other reason is that, in the past, we have asked the United States to contribute to what is the basis of peace and of defence – which is the balance of forces in Europe. That balance of forces is between the Soviet Union and its allies on one side, and the United States and its allies on the other. You don't imagine that balance as between the Soviet Union and Western European countries, quite apart from the difficult problem of nuclear forces vis-à-vis the German Federal Republic.

CHARLTON: So the American guarantee to Europe is still indispensable?

COUVE DE MURVILLE: Well, I don't think it *is* a guarantee. I think we have an alliance with the United States and that both of us have an interest to keep that alliance. We, to establish the balance of forces vis-à-vis the Soviet Union; and the United States, not to allow the Soviet Union to put itself in a position to invade Western Europe, and so destroy the balance of forces between the *Soviet Union* and the *United States*.

CHARLTON: But when you envisage the possibility of European 'co-operation' on defences in space – what *are* the possibilities?

COUVE DE MURVILLE: In several years things will be more clear. We will know what is required in the field of science, and what the European countries – each on its own or all together – are capable of doing. Only when we know that will we have a way of approaching the problem.

CHARLTON: When it comes to the possible development of a 'European personality' – a 'European Europe' in defence matters – is British failure in the past to do more in co-operation with France in these nuclear matters an impediment to that?

COUVE DE MURVILLE: The only answer, I think, is that we shall see. It's very difficult at present, not knowing exactly what the SDI is all about, to say what kind of co-operation could exist between the United Kingdom and France. You see in the past what the obstacle was: that you, the British, had a choice to make between the French and the Americans, and you made the choice of the Americans. Nobody can say if in two, or five, or ten years you will not have the same choice to make, whether the Americans will not ask you to work deeply with them in this IDS business.

CHARLTON: May I quote something that, from your memoirs, we know you told President Kennedy in May 1963? You said this: 'Nuclear co-operation with the United Kingdom was not a practical possibility, but it was not ruled out in principle.' Would you give the same answer today?

COUVE DE MURVILLE: Yes. I think it's not a practical system because the United Kingdom and the United States have close co-operation between them on that. If the conditions are changed, and if there is a common interest on both sides, in London and in Paris, then I don't see any reason why we shouldn't envisage a kind of co-operation between the French and the British in this field, as well as later on on the IDS itself.

CHARLTON: But, if that choice is faced again, do you believe the situation has evolved in any important way? After all, the British are now members of the European Community.

COUVE DE MURVILLE: Yes, I think to some extent the situation has changed. The British are closer to the Europeans since they are in the Common Market. And we are also much further from the War, and the War had been the closest co-operation between the British and the Americans. Twenty years ago the spirit of that co-operation was still very much alive.

MAURICE COUVE DE MURVILLE, THE FORMER Foreign Minister and Prime Minister when General de Gaulle was President of France, confirms the likelihood that the SDI will raise another assessment of where the future of the Anglo-American relationship lies. Is it to be in deeper British participation in Europe, or in maintaining a degree of American-British exclusivity? It is apparent that once more Britain will face some kind of choice.

Among the greatest of Europe's achievements since World War II has been the reconciliation of France and Germany. This relationship has been the motor of European unity. Two years ago Helmut Schmidt, the West German Chancellor from 1974 to 1982, concluded that new steps had to be taken if Western Europe were to remain a vital economic area. He called for a joint German and French industrial programme and suggested that West Germany help to pay for the expanded conventional armament of France, and that France consider extending her nuclear guarantee to cover West Germany. The former German Chancellor has argued strongly against the intention of the West German Government to participate in the American 'Star Wars' programme. In deciding that the SDI challenge should fall within the compass of renewed endeavours towards a European unity of purpose, to what extent does Helmut Schmidt consider that defence co-operation should become closer than hitherto between France and Germany?

HELMUT SCHMIDT: Well, not only as a consequence of SDI. I have been an advocate of close co-operation between the French and the Germans for almost twenty years. I was born and raised as an Anglophile. But I was disappointed by British policies vis-à-vis Europe and the EEC in its early stages. I then came to think that the power and the leadership of the United States was inevitable. Later on (and I am now sixty-seven), over thirty years as an active and operative political animal, I did understand that the interests of the Germans would be served best in close co-operation with the French. Or, in other words, all that the Germans desire – for instance, an honoured place in the international society; a normal relationship with the nations in Eastern Europe; the desire of ultimately getting the two parts of Germany together again (or, at least, to get the two parts of Germany under one and the same roof again) – can only happen, if ever, in so far as it is accepted by the French. The French acceptance of German strategic goals is the necessary legitimation; without that legitimation, it will never, it *could* never, happen. An American legitimation does not work in Europe. A British legitimation may work, but isn't that worthwhile. A French legitimation is what really matters.

CHARLTON: And therefore, an unconditional alliance with France is indispensable, as you see it, to the future of Europe?

HELMUT SCHMIDT: I would not subscribe to the word 'unconditional', I would not even in *marriage* subscribe to such a qualification. But an alliance with France, yes. And this would then, of course, also have to include specific hard-core co-operation in the military and defence field. Yes.

CHARLTON: But with something like the SDI on the agenda, a potentially vast new dimension which might cause us to revise all the horizons of strategic thinking so far – would you agree – do you think – that the question of how to extend French deterrence to Germany is likely to arise again under this kind of pressure, as it did with Adenauer and de Gaulle, for example, in the 1960s?

HELMUT SCHMIDT: It is not very likely, but the likelihood is growing in France. But please let me make a very important 'caveat' here. The *real* imbalance between East and Western Europe so far is *not* in the nuclear field; the real imbalance is in the field of mobilisable, *conventional* power. It is mostly in *this* field that I miss the close co-operation of French forces. There is no draft in England (there hasn't been conscription there for thirty years or more), there is no draft in America. You don't have reserves. If you want to call out reserves it would take you between one and two years; let's say it would take twenty-four months before you can arrive on the battlefield with substantial additional numbers. The German Army, were it to be mobilised, could be brought up within a week to far beyond a million men under arms. This is the most important thing that *ought* to be done also on the French side. Extending the area which is to be defended by the *nuclear force de frappe* is something which the French think is very important, but they have grave hesitations to do so (although the hesitation is withering a little). But, from a German point of view, this is more a psychological thing than a thing of military importance.

CHARLTON: Are future developments in this respect likely to include new kinds of responsibilities for the Federal Republic of Germany?

HELMUT SCHMIDT: I hope not. I hope not. If my country does appear as assuming some role in the nuclear field, whether it is strategic, or tactical or in between – (I hate these terms, by the way. If somebody kills me with a tactical weapon, he kills me, and this I understand to be strategic – because my own life, and the life of my nation, is of strategic value for a German leader! If you kill the German nation, either side, by tactical nuclear weapons, it is a *strategic* change to the composition of Europe and the world) – it would be detrimental to Germany's interest if Germany could be accused of taking up a role in the nuclear field. It should not do so.

CHARLTON: But would that rule out a possible sharing of certain systems under 'double-key' arrangements?

HELMUT SCHMIDT: No. A 'double-key' arrangement is something different again. Double-key may mean a sort of competence to say 'no', not necessarily a competence to say 'yes'. It does not necessarily mean giving away some positive power of disposing of weapons. 'Double-key' is an unclear term. What do you mean, sir, by using that word?

CHARLTON: I was going to suggest that the situation already exists with the F-104 Starfighter, which carries, or can carry, American nuclear weapons but which is flown by German crews. There is a capacity to say 'no' there?

HELMUT SCHMIDT: Oh, yes. I was always aware of that.

CHARLTON: Why not with Cruise and Pershing?

HELMUT SCHMIDT: They are not manned – most of them are not manned – by German soldiers. They are manned by Americans. So this *factual* 'double-key', of which you're talking, may not be the case there. It's different compared with the 104s or the Tornados.

CHARLTON: Just to be quite clear about this, if something of a *de facto* double-key system (the German capacity to say 'no') exists, with the Starfighter for example, might it also come to exist with a battlefield nuclear weapon – like the French Pluton? Do you see co-operation with France going as far as that?

HELMUT SCHMIDT: You know all this is *theoretical* strategy. Let us think of an *actual* situation. Let's assume a picture of a battle in which somebody in the West wishes, for the first time in that war, to use nuclear weapons against the attacker. Call them tactical, call them strategic, I don't mind. If you destroy Warsaw it is not a tactical move. It is a strategic move. If you throw nuclear bombs on the bridges by the River Vistula, or the River Oder, it is *not* just a tactical thing. You need to be a general to believe that it would be only a tactical move. It is a new quality.

If you introduce the nuclear quality into actual warfare (as opposed to intellectual games), and thereby kill some tens of thousands of people – how many soldiers on the side of the nation who has suffered these thousands of deaths would still be willing to fight, sir? This is a question which neither the NATO generals, nor the French, have asked themselves thoroughly enough. It is a ridiculous illusion to believe that, for instance, the German Bundeswehr will still fight on after you have eradicated Nuremberg or Frankfurt or some other city. It is nonsense. It will not work. It works only in the minds of intellectuals in our defence ministries, whether they be in Washington, or Paris, or London, or Bonn. Myself, having been a soldier in the last War, I know that soldiers can suffer. I know that there are some nations whose soldiers can suffer more than others. The Russians are great sufferers; they even have a passion for suffering, through all their history. But there are limits. If you start destroying the life of one's nation by so-called *tactical* nuclear weapons, destroying life by the tens of thousands, then they will not fight on. Therefore, to believe this is a possible line of actual defence is an illusion.

This insight will grow in Europe. The debate is no longer as it was in the 1960s. Then it was a strategic debate between three dozen or so members of the international defence community. Nowadays it is a debate in which bishops and priests and professors and laymen of all kinds participate. And it will broaden. And the doubts about the practicability of such a strategy will grow. I would foresee that one of the governing principles for laying down strategy will be the acceptability of that strategy to one's own nation.

IN THESE LAST OBSERVATIONS, Helmut Schmidt embraces such fundamental doubts about the long-standing NATO strategy of 'flexible response' (the early recourse to nuclear weapons in the event that conventional forces fail to halt a Soviet advance) as those raised for us (in the first chapter) by Robert McNamara when he said, 'I did not find . . . and I have never seen since, any indication that anyone in the world knows how to initiate the use of nuclear weapons with advantage to NATO.' They are doubts which the former German Chancellor – and the presumed battlefield is his, in Germany – believes call for greater conventional forces with which to man the ramparts of the West. But such doubts are also part of that 'curve of eroding nuclear stability' – and confidence therefore, in nuclear deterrence – which those of President Reagan's advisers who are proponents of strategic defence believe to be the wisdom of the SDI. And as the nature of strategic defence itself casts doubt on the efficacy of the NATO doctrine of 'flexible response', so on two counts the SDI would appear to hasten consideration of the choices Helmut Schmidt believes we must face.

The new German enthusiasm for defence co-operation with France, exemplified by Helmut Schmidt, has been answered by a French willingness to discuss a larger number of nuclear issues than at any previous time, and it is evidence of a political shift in France towards entertaining a closer military collaboration with Germany. In this sense, the basis for a new combination in the centre of Europe exists. Within the European Community, where she has still really to establish her political place, the pressure, therefore, grows on Britain to declare her hand in the development of a European defence personality. Should it take the form of 'institutionalising a difference' with the United States? This poses an old problem as far as Britain is concerned – the relationship between Europe and America as a whole.

EDWARD HEATH: France and Germany have a very close relationship which really dates back to the Adenauer-de Gaulle reconciliation at Reims. I've always welcomed this. But then I have worked for Britain to become a member of the Community so that we could be part of that reconciliation. It was not intended that it could be an axis which would exclude other countries. The strain in Europe comes if France and Germany appear to be trying to run the Community on their own – or developing in new directions, including defence and procurement, without jointly working with other countries. Our problem will be if we are not prepared to go wholeheartedly *with* them in Europe in the field of procurement and defence. My view is a very clear one: we should be prepared to go wholeheartedly with them in both of those fields.

CHARLTON: How is America going to like it? Isn't that a crucial question?

EDWARD HEATH: Well, you can't judge international affairs on whether you like it or not. President Kennedy said to me in 1962, 'My view of the Atlantic Alliance is of two tall equal pillars, one on each side of the Atlantic.' 'But', I said, 'you are a tall pillar – a strong pillar – and we in Europe are a short and rather shaky pillar.' He said, 'Yes, but I want Britain *in* for that very reason – to make a tall, strong pillar in Europe. And that will be an Alliance.' I agree with that concept and so do most people in Europe. But when you get to that stage (and this is what I didn't say to the President), then you get a *different* relationship; because it is a relationship of *equal* partners. It is the same in a firm. If you have one person who owns the greater part of it, it is a very hierarchical establishment. When you have equal partners running a show, then it is entirely different. Then it has to be consultation, co-ordination and co-operation. This is what has to be recognised on both sides of the Atlantic. It is when that philosophy is not maintained that you get the strains and the difficulties.

CHARLTON: Let me quote to you what you said in your Godkin Lectures at Harvard in the 1960s:

> I do not myself think it realistic to suppose that defence will be excluded indefinitely from the European experiment . . . It is unlikely that after spending so much money and skill either Britain or France will simply allow their nuclear forces to wither away and return to complete reliance on the United States deterrent. The idea of a European defence system might prove highly attractive to them.

In the light of the Strategic Defence Initiative, which in the opinion of many would at least mitigate the value of a small deterrent force, how does that issue of the two deterrent forces, British and French, present itself now when it comes to talking about a 'European defence personality'?

EDWARD HEATH: My argument is that we ought to do everything possible to get an agreement about the *non-establishment* of SDI forces between the two superpowers, and between the rest of us for that matter. Then, of course, the predicament is not as great as it might at first sight appear.

Because what I am saying is that we in Europe *must maintain our nuclear forces*. The French have got their own resources for producing it without any American assistance. It may be that – in the past, through various ways – they did get American knowledge and help, but it is their own force. As far as we are concerned, we are capable of providing basic essentials of that force ourselves; and we could, if necessary, develop our own way again. I think it is very necessary that Europe must maintain its own force, or some of the countries in Europe maintain that force. Of course, there was always the argument about Germany being involved in it, and it was said that Germany would then have its 'finger on the trigger'. That was never the proposal. It would mean that Germany could have its finger on the *safety-catch* the whole time; but nobody would be allowed to have their finger *alone* on the trigger.

CHARLTON: Do you see, as one possible series of developments, the idea of 'double-key arrangements' which would mean that there would be a development in German defence policy?

EDWARD HEATH: That is certainly possible. I think we've got to ask people to be more rational about these things forty years after the Second World War, and look to the future and the defence of the continent as far as the Soviet Union is concerned.

CHARLTON: If I may say so, your Godkin Lectures in 1967 have forecast the situation which might develop in the 1980s. We find you saying this:

> . . . whether or not Europe would need its own anti-ballistic missile system cannot be predicted now. If these systems *are* developed, we may be at the start of a new lap in the arms race between the United States and the Soviet Union, the implications of which for the allies of either power cannot now be foreseen . . .

Now, supposing the Russians and the Americans *do* come to some agreement to modify the Anti-Ballistic Missile Treaty of 1972, in order to allow the development of new technologies, how would you answer your own question that you posed in the 1960s at Harvard?

EDWARD HEATH: This is still, I think, a debatable point, exactly how far you can go in the Anti-Ballistic Missile Agreement. Even the experts differ on how much research is permitted, whether it can be a 'national' affair, or a 'one-city' affair, and so on. I think we ought to insist on the strictest possible interpretation of the ABM agreement.

Then, I think the next part of the argument is, if this *did* develop in the United States, if the United States did feel that it had a system which made the United States entirely safe, it could well be that an administration, or the Congress, could take the view that Europe was no longer of any consequence. In that case Europe would either have to be almost entirely defenceless (in the nuclear field at any rate) against the Soviet bloc, or else it would have to develop its nuclear defence still further. But it would *have to have that deterrent* against the Soviet bloc.

THE HISTORY OF PAST EFFORTS at military integration, like the European Defence Community of the 1950s, does not suggest encouraging precedents. But sovereignty is where sovereignty lies. A new debate has only just begun. The extent to which concepts like 'Star Wars' will further modify the prejudices of the nation states of Western Europe, whether they will continue to stand on the ancient ways that once made for safe advance, remains difficult to predict – and, of course, too early to say. The overwhelming case for the British deterrent, accepted by all British governments in the past, has been sovereignty, in the last resort. If the men in the Politburo thought the Americans might not come to the aid of Europe – if there was a 'weak' President, or an atmosphere of retreat in the United States – then the deterrent effect of American weapons would be useless. There follows the need for an independent deterrent, a second centre of decision, which in effect would couple the United States to the defence of Europe.

In the new circumstances which arise if strategic defence looks more feasible, the arguments point, unhelpfully, in different directions. In the uncertainties created if Soviet 'Star Wars' defences were to be put in place, or the Anti-Ballistic Missile Treaty were abrogated, the case in Britain for the Trident submarine, with its superior penetrating powers over the Polaris, would appear strengthened while, at the same time, leaving the future of deterrence in doubt. Britain, having taken the decision to modernise its nuclear deterrent with Trident, and at very great cost, would be buying a weapon system which the seller, the United States, has undertaken to render 'impotent' and 'obsolete'. When Trident was discussed and decided upon by Britain, a major advance in strategic defence was neither in prospect nor under consideration. If the strategic ballistic missile is indeed heading for obsolescence, it might be argued that Britain's defence effort should be concentrated on helping to create a greater conventional force in Europe, this being the real imbalance of power in Europe as between East and West in the eyes of Helmut Schmidt.

HELMUT SCHMIDT: The Europeans have to understand that it is beyond their reach, by their own means, to come up with a sufficient counterweight against the Soviet strategic means of nuclear warfare. But the Europeans *could* come up with enough military power to balance off all the power that the Soviet Union could muster in the sub-nuclear fields. Now, why don't they *do* it? What it needs is clarity in the minds of political leaders in Paris, Bonn, and in some other places. What is missing most is clarity in the minds of the leaders – not the number of study groups or academic symposia. We've had enough of them!

CHARLTON: What should be the political aim of such an endeavour? Would it be to forestall a divergence from the United States or to prepare for it?

HELMUT SCHMIDT: No. Neither. You know, 'divergence between Europe and the US', or 'crisis in NATO' – I've heard this over almost thirty-five years. It's a perennial headline in European newspapers. But despite all this scepticism, all these false prognoses, all this pessimism, the Alliance has not split up and it will not. It will not because even the most dumb leader in Europe or America understands that he, or she, cannot defend his or her country alone. And this view will prevail. I do not see any basic danger for the cohesion of the military alliance. What I *do* see right now is a diversion of strategic thinking and an enormous lack of leadership by the leaders.

CHARLTON: But this gap in strategic thinking has been opened up. How important is it, in your view, to close it?

HELMUT SCHMIDT: It would be important to close it. It could be closed partially by an act of will in Paris. Basically and comprehensively it can be closed only by the Americans.

CHARLTON: How could it be 'closed in Paris'?

HELMUT SCHMIDT: If, for instance, a French President would come to the decision that his forces and German forces should join each other – and that (in order to decorate it, psychologically) he would extend the area of defence for his *force de frappe* towards the River Elbe, or something like that. This would do most of the trick. If on top of all that he would also make clear that, although France will retain its own nuclear strategic force, nevertheless it is willing to acknowledge the necessity of the Americans to maintain the overall strategic balance with the Soviet forces, this would be enough. But it takes an act of will in Paris. It is, of course, against the very heavy psychological weight of the heritage of 'le Grand Charles'. Charles de Gaulle was such an outstanding person and he has influenced the thinking of everybody in France since his time. He has been gone for almost seventeen years now. But still, M. Mitterand, M. Chirac, M. Raymond Barre – there is some exception in the case of Valéry Giscard d'Estaing – still most of them are on de Gaulle's lines, that is, to enable France to defend herself against attacks from *any* direction of the skies. Do you remember that phrase?

CHARLTON: '*Tous Azimuts*'?

HELMUT SCHMIDT: *Ja.*

CHARLTON: Is a specifically European defence role conceivable to you, or useful?

HELMUT SCHMIDT: Oh yes, oh yes, it is. Let's assume that the French and the Germans plus Benelux join their forces. Let's assume also that some 35,000 British troops, if you so wish, join these forces. Put them all under French high command. It would work. It would make quite an impression on Marshal Ogarkov[2] and on his successors, and it would have a greater deterrence effect than all this bloody nonsense about 'Star Wars'.

THESE ARE THE FRUSTRATIONS of a Western Europe reduced in political efficacy by its own incapacity, sceptical about the technical possibility of

---

[2] Marshal N. V. Ogarkov, former Chief of the Soviet General Staff and subsequently (after the shooting down of the Korean airliner Flight 007) 'appointed' Commander in Chief of Warsaw Pact forces

disinventing the Bomb and realising the President's dream, worried about its cost. The Western Alliance has celebrated forty successful years and has ridden all its storms. But these are the attitudes which reflect the long-term strains within it. They are concentrated today upon a growing economic divergence of Europe and America, and upon differing perceptions of the quality of the Soviet threat. It is in this last field – with the unique privileges of shared intelligence, together with nuclear co-operation – that Britain enjoys that part of the 'special relationship' with the United States that now remains. Today America's special relationship based on *power* is with Germany and, concerning the Anglo-American special relationship, the former German Chancellor is almost dismissive. Echoing Dickens' description of Mr Squeers in *Nicholas Nickleby*, Helmut Schmidt observes that NATO has 'only one eye, when the popular prejudice runs in favour of two . . .'

HELMUT SCHMIDT: I have a very clear conviction. I have been co-operating with four American Presidents, one after the other during my time, and with I don't know how many US Defence Secretaries, quite outstanding personalities among them. But the interpretation of what is in the strategic interest of the United States – or what is in the strategic interest of the West in general – has changed quite often. Due to the prevailing interpretation of the day, they manipulated their photographs by satellite photography. They manipulated the data that they had available, and arranged the presentations in a way that suited the prevailing strategic doctrine. So I would like to make Europe itself as independent as possible as regards fact-finding. Europe ought to have its *own* monitoring satellites, and this we could easily do. Why don't we *do* it? We ought to be independent from the different interpretations and from the selectivity with which we are being informed (by differing, changing personalities, for instance, in the Pentagon, or in the CIA).

CHARLTON: Should the British be encouraged to sacrifice that element of the 'special relationship' which is left to them, the nuclear and intelligence relationship with the United States? Should we reconsider that, in favour of a Western European grouping in which we would carry less real weight than either West Germany or France?

HELMUT SCHMIDT: I don't know. I think this is a question that from time to time comes up in London, but doesn't really bother the continental Europeans. The continental Europeans have the feeling that the so-called 'special relationship' is indeed very special because it's a unilateral, not a bilateral thing. The *British* talk of a special relationship, not the people in the White House. They only use the phrase when they come to visit Westminster. Otherwise, it does not prevail in their feeling of the situation.

AMERICA AND BRITAIN CONTINUE to share intimately a broad strategic common ground, but the special relationship reflected at the outset a reciprocal capacity. Britain's reduced military power and the slow but steady decline in its economic ranking lie at the heart of a shift in the balance of that relationship which is dictated by basic facts of power and interest. Britain faces severe financial problems in keeping the Rhine Army up to strength, in modernising arms and equipment for its forces, and in making the change to the new nuclear deterrent force which is being built around the Trident submarine. 'Star Wars' dramatises the logic that Europe simply cannot go on doing, as nation states, all that needs to be done. The Europeans live in the shadow of the last expansionist empire on their continent. Will their concern at the temptation the 'Star Wars' technology might offer the Americans – to seek freedom from the burden of 'equal risk' which the Alliance imposes – make defence the agent which reanimates the ideas of European unity, the rediscovery of the path of integration laid down forty years ago?

EDWARD HEATH: I have long held that it is a necessity. It's an historical necessity. Your question was, will *this* itself create the momentum in the European Economic Community? I do not think so. I think that to do that we've got to carry the creation of a completely free market much further. We have to remove internal barriers to trade and activities of all kinds. But, having recreated that momentum, then we shall have the means of carrying on further in the defence and procurement field in a way which I have described. So the two are interlocked. After all, when I gave the Godkin Lectures at Harvard in 1967, we'd still got tremendous momentum in the Community. Many foresaw that if Britain, Denmark and Ireland joined it would help that momentum. Since then we have had world problems of high inflation and then mass unemployment; the Community has lost its momentum and we have got to get it back. When ordinary people feel that it means something to them, then we shall get their support also for defence and procurement.

CHARLTON: But when you add up in your own mind the possibilities the SDI moderates or advances, the new directions it's likely to confirm or deny, do you see the independence of Europe on the rise and 'Atlanticism' in decline?

EDWARD HEATH: I see Atlanticism in decline, but I can't say that I see Europe 'on the rise'. If one judges Atlanticism by practical achievements and not just conference communiqués, then I have been dismayed by these past few years. If one asks, is Europe taking a grip on the situation *because* of it, the plain and truthful answer must also be no, it isn't.

THE UNITED STATES HAS TURNED TO SPACE in order to turn a tide. It still lags behind the Soviet Union in some nuclear offensive weapons (such as land-based missiles) and civil and air defence. In addition, the Soviet Union is making offensive missiles at a faster pace than the US and is constantly strengthening its conventional forces. There is evidence that it has redoubled its long and persistent efforts to develop its own space weapons. With an anti-missile defence system as its shield and the offensive nuclear weapon as its sword, the United States would have a real military edge over the Soviet Union.

The principal beneficiaries of the ABM treaty in 1972 were undoubtedly Britain and France. A successful move now towards strategic defence by the United States and the Soviet Union would oblige them to expand very considerably their nuclear capacities, but attended always by the risk that if 'defence' really did become unbeatable (as President Reagan has willed that it should), then the British and French nuclear forces, on which huge amounts have been spent over some thirty years, would have reached a dead-end. Like Moscow, although undoubtedly for very different reasons, Paris and London prefer to continue to live in a system of deterrence based upon the threat of the ballistic missile.

But even if 'Star Wars' does, in the end, hold a shield above the heads of populations and geographical areas, it will not make them safe from attack. Western Europe, in particular, would have little defence against low-flying as opposed to ballistic missiles. Will the allies of the United States, therefore, have more to fear? If the Herculean technical demands of strategic defences can be met by the Soviet Union, the NATO strategy which calls for using nuclear weapons when necessary will be ineffective. This is the question which makes the SDI and strategic defence different in quality from the many 'nuclear' issues NATO has faced since its inception, as Lord Carrington, the Secretary General of the North Atlantic Treaty Organisation, and with a long experience in defence posts in the United Kingdom, readily agrees.

LORD CARRINGTON: This one in a way is a bit different, because over the last thirty-five years the offensive weapon has been all-powerful. Nobody has ever *thought* that it has been possible really to defend yourself against ballistic missiles. Even in the days of the ABM, nobody really supposed that it was going to be an adequate defence. Here you have something which is rather different in character. You have the offence catching up with the defence. Obviously that affects strategy.

CHARLTON: The United States is the leader of an alliance. In the past, advances, initiatives made by the United States have very often dictated choices. When you compare this choice with others the Alliance has been called upon to make in the past, how does it compare?

CARRINGTON: I don't think it is a choice. How it strikes me is this. If I were an American, and until recently my continent had been inviolable (it's only in the last ten to fifteen years or so that there has really been a threat to the North American continent, the homeland), it would seem perfectly natural to try to develop a defence against ballistic missiles. After all, anything that would stop a nuclear missile falling on your head would be a plus if you were an American. Indeed, it would be a plus if you were a European. It would be a plus for the world generally if you can do this sort of thing. Equally, supposing research leads to the ability to put up an inviolable umbrella over the United States and Western Europe, then there are all sorts of strategic consequences which I think we would have to consider very carefully. I think this is the element which worries the Europeans. I think it is as natural for the Europeans to be worried about the consequences as it is natural for the Americans to wish to do it.

Now if you take the 'ultimate', that is to say that you *could* actually devise a system in which no ballistic missiles could reach the United States, or indeed Western Europe, and the Soviet Union did *not* have that system, then obviously there is a considerable *superiority* on the part of a United States which is invulnerable. On the other hand, if the Soviet Union had the same system, then *everybody* is invulnerable to ballistic missiles. But, of course, they're *not* invulnerable to nuclear weapons delivered by other means. Nor is the deterrent to *conventional* war quite so easily seen as we see it at the present time. The SDI has no relevance whatsoever to manned bombers or Cruise missiles. In current circumstances, to try to attain superiority over the Soviet Union would probably lead to the Soviet Union either trying to match what the Americans did, or trying to gain superiority themselves. They may very well have been trying to do that anyway. But after all, enough is enough, I think – provided that the American and Western deterrent remains credible enough to deter war, I would not have thought there was a particular added margin of safety in trying to get superiority.

I think the difficulty really with the SDI lies in the deterrent to conventional war. Nowadays people are rather inclined to think that somehow or other conventional war is acceptable and nuclear war is unthinkable. But more than fifty million people were killed in the Second World War. I think we want to avoid a conventional war. I think the question for us is what would happen to the deterrence to both conventional war, and the deterrence to nuclear weapons carried by weapons other than ballistic missiles. That is the question nobody has yet really answered.

CHARLTON: Would you like to try to answer it? Given the developments in prospect, can 'deterrence' last?

CARRINGTON: I am not capable of making a judgment as to whether it is very likely that you *can* create circumstances in which a place the size of the United States and Western Europe *is* invulnerable. I would have thought it is going to be quite difficult. I think in the end we are going to be faced with a situation in which you can do it *up to a point*. I think probably deterrence is going to last because, however disagreeable the idea of deterrence is, it's a good deal better than the reality of war! I happen to believe that deterrence has proved successful in keeping the peace in this world. I would be very alarmed to see it go.

CHARLTON: What contribution do you see the SDI making to a feeling that we cannot expect to go on like this, living with the threat of mutual annihilation?

CARRINGTON: The whole concept of MAD, 'mutual assured destruction', is something which a lot of people do find incredible. I think people are groping for some other way of keeping the peace. But I remember that old cartoon in the First World War of those two guys under fire in the shell hole. One is saying to the other, 'If you knows of a better 'ole, go to it!'
CHARLTON: Bruce Bairnsfather's cartoon of his famous old sweat in the trenches, 'Old Bill'?
CARRINGTON: That's right. I think our problem is that we *don't* actually have a better hole to go to.

THE EUROPEANS HAVE RESTED THEIR FUTURE for so long on the American nuclear guarantee that they have virtually given up certain primary responsibilities, at least for their own defence. The guarantee to Europe depended on an American nuclear ascendancy over the Soviet Union, and this with the achievement of parity by the Russians is in question today. Unless the Russians and the Americans jointly agree to extend it, the Anti-Ballistic Missile Treaty will expire before the end of this decade; but the new technical possibilities of a strategic defence exist (a defence of weapons first, and perhaps of populations later). Contemporary history suggests they will be energetically pursued. This must cast doubt on whether the ABM treaty will be renewed, at least in its present form. Europe, therefore, faces the prospect of a defence of the continental United States (which was once abandoned) and an increase, in the short term, in Soviet offensive nuclear power. It is in this last respect that Helmut Schmidt, for many years Germany's Defence Minister and then Chancellor, reflects upon the considerations which prompted the Americans to take the initiative which led to the Anti-Ballistic Missile Treaty of 1972.

HELMUT SCHMIDT: It was possible to agree on such a limitation because both sides, by 1972, had done enough research and development (had even undertaken some production of the actual hardware) that they could understand that an unlimited arms race, in this field, might lead to the destabilisation of the strategic system which had governed the world so far – and was meant to govern the future also. I call that system the *balance* of nuclear capabilities – the balance of power. They realised that could become endangered.

Now, SDI is nothing new. It is the continuation of what the Soviet Union, as well as the United States, had undertaken since at least the middle of the 1960s. The impression has prevailed so far that it is only the United States of America that is pursuing so-called 'strategic defence'; that the Soviet Union, while criticising the Americans, is doing no such thing. That is a wrong impression. It would be correct to say that both of them, for almost twenty years, have carried on research and development in this field – sometimes with a different emphasis, sometimes a little stronger, sometimes a little weaker. It seems to me that, out of SALT I and SALT II and the ABM treaty (which is the most important of the three), basically the ABM treaty was (a) in the interests of the United States, and (b) to the same degree in the interests of the Soviet Union. It was also in the interests of the smaller nuclear powers like the United Kingdom, France, China. Limiting anti-ballistic missile defences to a small number of systems means that the relatively unsophisticated nuclear systems (of Britain, of France, of China) would retain their strategic values to some degree. If the ABM treaty goes, then the importance of the *force de frappe* as well as of the British deterrent will diminish. No doubt of that.

CHARLTON: Does the SDI alter the whole core of the debate as you see it? When it comes to European attitudes, will they not depend less on the American SDI programme but on Soviet responses to it at various stages of its development?

HELMUT SCHMIDT: The European fate depends for the most part on Europe's ability – in the *sub*-nuclear strategic areas – to come up with sufficient forces to balance off the Soviet superiority in numbers. I think the idea that you can defend yourselves by nuclear weapons will become less and less credible, less and less acceptable. If the people living in Glasgow, or living on the Downs in the south of England, or in Cornwall – if they lived where I live, in Hamburg, they would judge this in a much more realistic way. If I get into a car parked at my front door and drive eastwards, it takes me twenty-five minutes to get to what they call the Iron Curtain. If they let me pass, it would take me another thirty-five minutes to meet the first Soviet tank division. Well, vice versa, it takes *them* one hour to get from where they are to my front door. It takes their fighter bombers just five minutes. We live on the battlefield. We live on the ground that is seen as *the* battlefield by the planners in the West and the planners in the East. Therefore we find it a little bit more difficult to believe in being defended by dropping nuclear weapons on our homes. We need American strategic forces for the theoretically thinkable case of Soviet strategic nuclear threats against Western Europe, that's true. But the West will not use strategic nuclear capabilities against the Soviets if they take a city at the border.

CHARLTON: Victor Hugo said that there was no force more powerful in history than an idea whose time has come. Is strategic defence against the intercontinental ballistic missile an idea whose time has come?

HELMUT SCHMIDT: No, I don't think so. The idea has already been created in the 1960s under another, and less prestigious, name, and I don't see a breakthrough forthcoming. In particular, I do not see a situation in which the West has the means for a strategic breakthrough, and the East has not. There never has been a sweeping technical advantage in the military field for longer than three or four years. Sometimes the Russians had the advantage and we in the West lagged behind. That was true of 'Sputnik', which certainly was not just a scientific undertaking but, of course, a military one. I do not think the strategy of military 'balance' will be toppled. If we give up that idea of 'balance' it will also mean that we give up the idea of arms limitation as a whole. There is no future for arms limitation if somebody, be it in the Kremlin or be it in the White House, believes that he or she can make their country superior in the field of military arms to the other side. The idea of superiority will destroy the idea of arms limitation. So what I am saying is that I do not believe in a unilateral breakthrough. It is much more likely that, if a breakthrough is to happen, *both* sides will make the breakthrough. The period between now and the breakthrough is then a most dangerous one, because somebody who believes that he has an advantage, or an edge for some time, might be tempted to *take* advantage — to take chances. I believe in the will for equilibrium. Otherwise I would foresee a rather hostile and dangerous world.

HERE ARE SOME OF THE PRINCIPAL reasons why the Europeans would prefer the Russians and Americans to reach a joint agreement on the nature of the strategic relationship between East and West. It would release them from the rigours of the likely consequence of 'Star Wars' defences – the cost of doing more about defending themselves. This is the gap – not one of choice but of performance – that one sees opening up between Europe and America, with the Americans ready for another advance which the Europeans themselves cannot make or match. The familiar New World belief of President Reagan in American technology shows more confidence in its capacity to deliver us from the nuclear threat than it does in the axiom that stability in the nuclear age will continue to be based upon mutual vulnerability.

EDWARD HEATH: The Europeans are simply not prepared to see a vast quantity of Alliance resources poured into something which is going to lead to another stage in the arms race, yet more resources poured into it by the Soviet Union – all of which does nothing whatsoever to increase our safety. The argument that, if you have a defensive system, your safety is greater than with a deterrent system falls to the ground immediately you realise that no defensive system can be fool-proof. Therefore you have *still got to have the deterrent*. From that point of view I think the argument you're using is baseless.

I can remember the fuss when Mr Baldwin[3] said in 1935, I think, 'Of course, I can't guarantee that no German bomber will get through to this country . . .' Immediately the shouts went up. He was accused of being an incompetent Prime Minister, and the Government of not looking after the defence of the country and so on. Baldwin was speaking the absolute truth. Nobody *could* guarantee that no German bomber would get through to this country.

[3] Stanley Baldwin, British Prime Minister in 1923, 1924–29 and 1935–37

The same will be true of the SDI. And so, the answer is that this is *not* a brilliant new lead to the safety of the world. It is in fact an enormous expenditure on armaments – on top of a deterrent which already can destroy the world many, many times over. What is the point of that?

THUS THERE ARE POWERFUL ARGUMENTS to suggest that 'Star Wars' will produce as great a controversy as any in the history of the transatlantic alliance. It is more than a decade since Henry Kissinger drove out to the Politburo's private hunting retreat in Zavidovo, ninety miles north of Moscow, to spend the night shooting wild boar with Leonid Brezhnev, the leader of Soviet Russia. He was the first and only Westerner to be accorded this privilege, and it marked the high point of détente. Kissinger entertained the hope that the peace Brezhnev spoke of, in the stillness of that night and their hours alone, could become a genuine co-existence – that 'the boar hound and the boar' might 'pursue their pattern as before, but reconciled among the stars . . .'. In the fascinating chapter of his memoirs which records the glimpse of the Soviet hierarchy he had that night, Kissinger himself concluded that 'we can never know, and neither probably can the Soviet leaders'. But those who dominate, from office, the American strategic debate today believe that détente – and the American acceptance of parity in the strategic nuclear balance – emboldened the Soviet leaders to a more provocative opportunism. President Reagan, surely, would find little to dispute in Churchill's judgment at the height of the wartime alliance with the Soviet Union, in the months before the first great negotiation with Stalin's Russia at Yalta: 'I have tried in every way to put myself in sympathy with these Communist leaders, but facts and force are the only realities they understand.'

The Americans are trying to get the Russians to compromise in some critical areas. 'Star Wars' is risk. It is also opportunity. The time has come to talk to the Russians about the future. It is a platitude that there is a good deal of common ground. That neither side wants nuclear war, or wishes to commit suicide, is conceded by all our witnesses on all sides of the argument which, down the years, have shaped the American strategic debate. And (to balance the platitudes), neither side would accept defeat rather than *use* nuclear weapons. Therefore the corollary of the concept of 'decisive battle', which the advent of nuclear parity has abolished, is arms control negotiations. The history of the West's political debate suggests that without a credible arms control policy the United States will find difficulty in retaining the support of its allies, and that the Congress will not vote for adequate defence budgets to match the Soviet effort. But the Soviet Union appears to have understood the decade of the 1970s, of SALT and the emerging détente with the United States, as, in essence, a licence to exercise their growing strengths in areas where they had been relatively weak. In that sense, arms control agreements without restraints in political conduct have not contributed to peace. The notion of a permanent Soviet adversary who is not defeatable (because the terms for that defeat would not be acceptable), yet whose very Constitution, written by Lenin, means America harm, remains novel and uncomfortable. The evolution of the American debate reflects this fundamental unease: that 'doing business' with a defined, explicit adversary is an unnatural activity. To survey this unfolding debate in America from the 1970s into the 1980s is to see also the growing suspicion that, no matter how satisfactory Alliance defence looked to American or indeed Allied eyes, the United States was dealing with an adversary who *did* see some utility in military advantage at the margin – as with Harold Brown's 'When we build, they build – when we stop building, they build' during the Carter Presidency.

It is possible to measure the strategic balance in many different ways. But as it has declined, marginally, against the West, the United States has been asking more and more of its strategic forces. This is directly relevant to the SDI. What, then, is the SDI's contribution? It could possibly be many things. President Nixon, who together with Mr Brezhnev called into being the SALT agreement, was among the first to express a belief that strategic defence efforts are indispensable to arms control because 'without the SDI the Soviet Union will have no incentive to limit its offensive missiles.' The SDI can be designed to halt the retreat from 'assured destruction'; which is to say that *weapons* must remain invulnerable and *populations* undefended. And if command, control, and leadership can be defended, it would seem to strengthen the nuclear deterrence system which is in place today. The SDI does not yet exist. However, the inherent possibilities, sustained by historical awareness of the decisive role played by American technology in the past, have already shown themselves to be coercive.

In the breathtaking point of departure which emerged in the autumn of 1986 at the Reykjavik summit between President Reagan and Mr Gorbachev, the President – to the considerable perturbation of America's NATO allies – appeared to condone a proposal to eliminate all ballistic nuclear missiles by 1996, within a decade. Therefore, at Reykjavik the SDI was treated as a reality. In order to preserve his freedom to pursue something yet to be *achieved,* strategic defence through the SDI, the President seemed ready to sacrifice what have been regarded, for more than twenty years, as the invulnerable and indispensable instruments of what we *have* – nuclear deterrence, which is the essence of western security. Not the least of the paradoxes confronted in the haunted house at Reykjavik, where the two leaders met and finally broke on the issue without agreement, is that the SDI appears to have, in effect, preserved vital instruments and concepts of deterrence which the President in his 23 March 1983 speech believed it should supersede.

To the still uncertain extent that it is really serious political business, the 'star wars' concept puts a question mark against whatever benefit the Soviet Union considers has accrued to it from its strategic modernisation efforts of the last twenty years. In World War II Henry Kaiser's shipyards built ships faster than Hitler's U-boats could sink them. Similarly, the Russians could be contemplating obsolescence (if not the impotence) of their huge land-based force of heavy missiles before the end of the century. The Russians have to assume that the SDI is indeed real. But they can also look at the calendar and see that there are several Presidential elections, and many Congressional elections, between now and the possibility of escape from the terrestrial horizon of nuclear deterrence in the defence of populations and of homelands from space.

As yet we do not and we cannot know. The dialogue is, therefore, sure to be protracted. What the Soviet Union *does* know is that it is at the beginning of an enduring, though not necessarily permanent, technological disadvantage in striving for mastery of the highest of high defence technology. 'If you will begin in doubts, you may end in certainties' was the conclusion of that masterful Elizabethan, Francis Bacon. And, as he pointed out, the converse is equally true. But to consecrate the present has never been the American way.

THE CONTRIBUTORS

BONDI, Sir Hermann. Born 1919. British mathematician. Director General, European Space Research Organisation, Paris 1967–71; Chief Scientific Adviser to Ministry of Defence 1971–77; Chief Scientist, Department of Energy 1977–80; Master of Churchill College, Cambridge 1983–.

BROWN, Harold. Born 1927. American physicist and government official. Member, Scientific Advisory Commission on Ballistic Missiles to Secretary of Defence 1958–61; Secretary of Air Force 1965–69; President, California Institute of Technology 1969–77; Secretary of Defence 1977–81.

CARRINGTON, Lord (Peter). Born 1919. British politician. Parliamentary Secretary, Ministry of Defence 1954–56; First Lord of the Admiralty 1959–63; Leader of the Opposition, House of Lords 1964–70 and 1974–79; Secretary of State for Defence 1970–74; Foreign Secretary 1979–82; Secretary General, NATO 1984–.

CARTER, President Jimmy. Born 1924. American politician and farmer. Lt Cmdr, submarines and battleships, US Navy 1946–53; Georgia State Democratic Senator 1962–66; Governor of Georgia 1971–74; President of US 1977–81.

CARVER, Field Marshal Lord (Michael). Born 1915. British army officer. 7th Armoured Division 1939–45; Colonel, General Staff, Supreme HQ Allied Powers Europe 1951; Director of Plans, War Office 1958–59; Deputy Commander, UN Forces Cyprus 1964; Commander in Chief Far East 1967–69; Chief of General Staff 1971–73; Field Marshal 1973; Chief of Defence Staff 1973–76.

COUVE DE MURVILLE, Maurice. Born 1907. French diplomat and politician. French Committee of National Liberation (Algeria) 1943; French permanent representative, NATO 1954–55; Ambassador to US 1955–56; Ambassador to West Germany 1956–58; Minister of Foreign Affairs 1958–68; Prime Minister of France 1968–69.

HEATH, Rt Hon. Edward. Born 1916. British politician. War service 1939–45; Conservative MP 1950–; Joint Deputy Government Chief Whip 1952; Deputy Government Chief Whip 1953–55; Chief Whip

1955–59; Minister of Labour 1959–60; Lord Privy Seal with Foreign Office responsibilities 1960–63; Secretary of State for Industry, President of Board of Trade 1963–64; Leader of the Opposition 1965–70; Prime Minister of UK 1970–74; Leader of the Opposition 1974–75.

HOFFMAN, Fred S. American government official and economist. Staff member, Rand Corporation, studying problems of nuclear strategy and systems analysis 1950–65; Deputy Assistant Secretary of Defence, Systems Analysis 1965–67; Assistant Director, Budget Bureau 1967–69; Manager, Energy Policy Programme, Rand Corporation 1973–81; Chairman, 'Hoffman reports' on SDI for President Reagan.

JONES, General David. Born 1921. American Air Force officer. Operations Planner, Strategic Air Command HQ 1954; Aide to Commander in Chief, SAC 1955–57; Chief Strategic Divisional Operations, USAF HQ 1960–64; Inspector General, USAF HQ Europe 1965–67; Vice Commander, 7th Air Force, Vietnam 1969; Commander in Chief USAF, Germany 1971–74; Chief of Staff USAF 1974–78; Chairman, Joint Chiefs of Staff 1978–82.

KEYWORTH, Dr George. Born 1939. American scientist and government official. Physics staff member, Los Alamos National Laboratory 1968–73; Assistant Group Leader, Neutron Physics, Los Alamos 1973–74; Group Leader 1974–77; Physics Division Leader 1978–81; Acting Laser Fusion Division Leader 1980–81; Science Adviser to President Reagan 1981–85.

KISSINGER, Dr Henry. Born 1923 (Germany). American statesman and university professor. US Army Counter-Intelligence Corps 1943–46; Director, Study Group on Nuclear Weapons and Foreign Policy, Council of Foreign Relations 1955–56; Consultant, Weapons Systems Evaluation Group, Joint Chiefs of Staff 1956–60; National Security Council 1961–63; Professor of Government, Harvard University 1962–71; Assistant to US President for National Security Affairs 1969–75; Secretary of State 1973–77.

McNAMARA, Robert Strange. Born 1916. American government official and international civil servant. Assistant Professor of Business Administration, Harvard University 1940–43; USAF service in England, India, China and Pacific 1943–46; Ford Motor Company 1946–61, President 1960–61; Secretary of Defence 1961–68; President, World Bank 1968–81.

NITZE, Paul. Born 1907. American administrator and government official. Investment banker 1929–40; Vice Chairman, Strategic Bombing Survey 1944–46; Director, Policy Planning Staff, State Department 1950–53;

Assistant Defence Secretary, International Security Affairs 1961–63; Secretary of the Navy 1963–67; Deputy Secretary of Defence 1967–69; Member, US SALT Delegation 1969–74; Head, US Delegation to Intermediate-Range Nuclear Forces negotiations 1981–.

ODOM, General William. Born 1932. American army officer. US military liaison mission to Soviet Forces, Germany 1964–66; US Military Academy, West Point 1966–69, 1974–76; Army Attaché, US Embassy, Moscow 1972–74; White House National Security Staff member 1977–81; Assistant Chief of Staff for Intelligence 1981–85; Director, National Intelligence Agency 1985–.

PERLE, Richard. Born 1941. American government official. Post-graduate student, London School of Economics 1962–63; Consultant to Special Assistant, Defence Department 1969; Professional staff member, Senate National Security Subcommittee 1970–72; Professional staff member, permanent subcommittee on investigations, Senate Committee on Government Affairs 1973–80; Assistant Secretary for International Security Policy, Defence Department 1980–.

ROSTOW, Eugene. Born 1913. American lawyer, economist and government official. Assistant to Assistant Secretary of State (Dean Acheson) 1942–44; Assistant to Executive Secretary, UN Economic Commission for Europe, Geneva 1949–50; Dean, Yale University Law School 1955–65; Under Secretary of State for Political Affairs 1966–69; President, Atlantic Treaty Association 1973–76; Director, Arms Control and Disarmament Agency 1981–83.

RUSK, Dean. Born 1909. American government official. US Army 1940–46; Special Assistant to Secretary of War 1946; Deputy Under Secretary of State 1949–50; Assistant Secretary of State for Far Eastern Affairs 1950–51; Secretary of State 1961–69; Professor of International Law, University of Georgia 1971–.

SCHMIDT, Helmut. Born 1918. German politician and economist. German Army 1939–45; Manager of Transport Administration, State of Hamburg 1949–53; Vice-Chairman, Social Democratic Party 1968–84; Minister of Defence 1969–72; Minister of Finance and Economics 1972–74; German Chancellor 1974–82.

SCOWCROFT, Lt-General Brent. Born 1925. American Air Force officer and government official. Assistant Professor of Russian History, US Military Academy, West Point 1953–57; Assistant Air Attaché, US Embassy, Belgrade 1959–61; Associate Professor of Political Science, USAF Academy, Colorado 1962–63, Department Head 1963–64;

Various national security posts with Defence Department 1968–72; Military Assistant to the President, White House 1972; Deputy Assistant and Assistant to President for National Security Affairs 1973–77; Member, President's General Advisory Committee on Arms Control 1977–81; Chairman, Presidential Commission on Strategic Forces 1983–.

SMITH, Gerard. Born 1914. American government official and lawyer. US Navy 1941–45; Special Assistant, US Atomic Energy Commission 1950–54; Special Assistant to Secretary of State for Atomic Affairs 1954–57; Deputy Chief, US Delegation to International Atomic Energy Agency Treaty negotiations 1955–56; Chief US political adviser, Atoms for Peace Conference; Chief Aide to Secretary of State, London Disarmament Conference 1957; Assistant Secretary of State and Director, Policy Planning, State Department 1957–61; Director, US Arms Control and Disarmament Agency 1968–72; Head, US SALT Delegation, Helsinki and Vienna 1969–72; Ambassador-at-large 1977–.

SONNENFELDT, Helmut. Born 1926 (Germany). American government official. US Army Counter-Intelligence Corps; State Department 1952–59; Policy Officer, US Disarmament Administration 1960–61; Director, Office of Research and Analysis for USSR and Eastern Europe 1966–69; Senior Staff member for Europe and East–West Relations, National Security Council 1969–74; Counsellor, State Department 1974–77; School of Advanced International Studies, Johns Hopkins University 1977–.

TELLER, Dr Edward. Born 1908 (Hungary). American scientist. Research Associate, Göttingen 1931–33; Lecturer, University of London 1934–35; Professor of Physics, George Washington University 1935–41; Professor of Physics, Columbia University 1941–42; Physicist, Manhattan Engineer District 1942–46; Los Alamos Scientific Laboratory 1943–46; Professor of Physics, University of Chicago 1946–52; Assistant Director, Los Alamos 1949–52; Consultant (Livermore Branch), Lawrence Radiation Laboratory 1952–53, Director 1958–60; Associate Director, Lawrence Livermore Radiation Laboratory 1954–75 (now Emeritus); Professor of Physics, University of California 1953–60, (Berkeley) 1960–71, University Professor 1971–75 (now Emeritus); Senior Research Fellow, Hoover Institution 1975–.

WEINBERGER, Caspar. Born 1917. American government official. US Army 1941–45; Member, California State Legislature 1952–58; Vice Chairman and Chairman, California Republican Central Committee 1960–64; California State Director of Finance 1968–79; Deputy Director, Federal Office of Management and Budget 1970–72; Secretary of Health, Education and Welfare 1973–75; Secretary of Defence 1981–.

INDEX